CHICAGO
The Delaplaine
2020 Long Weekend Guide

Andrew Delaplaine

GET 3 FREE NOVELS
Like political thrillers?
See next page to download 3 FREE page-turning
novels—no strings attached.

**NO BUSINESS HAS PAID A SINGLE PENNY OR GIVEN _ANYTHING_
TO BE INCLUDED IN THIS BOOK.**

Chicago Editor: **Robert Vandal**
Senior Editors - ***Renee & Sophie Delaplaine***
Senior Writer - **James Cubby**

Gramercy Park Press
New York – London – Paris

Copyright © by Gramercy Park Press - All rights reserved.

WANT 3 **FREE** THRILLERS?
Why, of course you do!
If you like these writers--
Vince Flynn, Brad Thor, Tom Clancy, James Patterson, David Baldacci, John Grisham, Brad Meltzer, Daniel Silva, Don DeLillo
If you like these TV series –
House of Cards, Scandal, West Wing, The Good Wife, Madam Secretary, Designated Survivor

---

You'll love the **unputdownable** series about Jack Houston St. Clair, with political intrigue, romance, and loads of action and suspense.

Besides writing travel books, I've written political thrillers for many years that have delighted hundreds of thousands of readers. I want to introduce you to my work!
Send me an email and I'll send you a link where you can download the first 3 books in my bestselling series, absolutely FREE.

Mention **this book** when you email me.
andrewdelaplaine@mac.com

CHICAGO
The Delaplaine Long Weekend Guide

TABLE OF CONTENTS

Chapter 1 – WHY CHICAGO? – 4

Chapter 2 – GETTING ABOUT – 10

Chapter 3 – WHERE TO STAY – 14
High on the Hog – Sensible Alternatives – On a Budget

Chapter 4 – WHERE TO EAT – 27

Chapter 5 – NIGHTLIFE – 77

Chapter 6 – WHAT TO SEE & DO – 91

Chapter 7 – SHOPPING & SERVICES – 118

INDEX – 125

Chapter 1
WHY CHICAGO?

What a wonderful town, Chicagoland.

I couldn't believe the place when I first saw it. I was coming from New York (back in the '70s) in fine weather in early summer. It was night. I took a cab into town and walked up the Magnificent Mile in awe. Ladies and gentlemen walked down the street arm-in-arm, actually promenading.

There was grass on Michigan Avenue. Real grass. I reached down and touched it. You wouldn't find grass like that on Fifth Avenue. No, sir.

There was an electricity in the air in Chicago I noticed that very first night. And I've always been aware of it. There's that same sense in New York, of course, a sensation of excitement, of swiftness, of opportunity—*of hustle*—but somehow it was different here in Chicago. The pace here has slightly less of an edge to it. The people are nicer. They are polite. They are not rude, crude or rough. Maybe the word I'm looking for is *Normal.* It's that Midwest upbringing, I tell myself, and that must be it. This may be the City of Big Shoulders, but the people inhabiting it are as nice as the farmers plowing fields 300 miles away. (Well, there are certain neighborhoods....)

That first night I spent sleeping on the floor of our branch office at the corner of Oak and Rush, which I found out later was quite an exciting corner with a fascinating history. When I woke up in the morning and looked out of the floor-to-ceiling windows, I saw people swimming in the lake.

Swimming!
In the lake. In the 1970s!
I was aghast.

Back in New York, you wouldn't dip your toe in the Hudson River or the East River.

That was then. This is now. Now they're harvesting oysters from beds in the East River.

I remember running down and asking a cop how people could swim in the filthy water. He explained that the river flowing into the lake had been reversed. The river flowed *backwards!* The water was clean.

I couldn't believe it.

But this was just the beginning of a long love affair with Chicago. There's nothing not to like about this town—except the freezing wind that comes off the lake in the wintertime.

A couple of years later, in February, I was having a business lunch at the top of the **Hancock Tower** in what is now called the **Signature Room**. A blizzard blew snow off the lake so hard the snow moved horizontally, not vertically. Looking over the shoulder of the person opposite me, I saw the building swaying. I didn't know if the Hancock Tower was swaying or the building I was looking at. I am not an engineer. I just knew this was no place for a Southern boy.

After lunch, my head bent down, I made my way back to my office and announced to the staff that the Editorial Department of our travel magazine (that would be me) was moving to our offices in Miami, at least for the winter months.

I've returned dozens of times, of course—even in February—and the simple truth is that whether it's winter, summer, spring or fall, there's no place like this Toddlin' Town.

Before we get into the nitty-gritty, I'm reprinting Carl Sanders's famous poem "Chicago," first published I think in 1914. It captures the city like no other verse ever written.

HOG Butcher for the World,
   Tool Maker, Stacker of Wheat,
   Player with Railroads and the Nation's Freight Handler;
   Stormy, husky, brawling,
   City of the Big Shoulders:
      They tell me you are wicked and I believe them, for

    I have seen your painted women under the gas lamps
       luring the farm boys.
And they tell me you are crooked and I answer: Yes, it
       is true I have seen the gunman kill and go free to
       kill again.
And they tell me you are brutal and my reply is: On the
       faces of women and children I have seen the marks
       of wanton hunger.
And having answered so I turn once more to those who
       sneer at this my city, and I give them back the sneer
       and say to them:
Come and show me another city with lifted head singing
       so proud to be alive and coarse and strong and cunning.
Flinging magnetic curses amid the toil of piling job on
       job, here is a tall bold slugger set vivid against the
       little soft cities;
Fierce as a dog with tongue lapping for action, cunning
       as a savage pitted against the wilderness,
          Bareheaded,
          Shoveling,
          Wrecking,
          Planning,
          Building, breaking, rebuilding,
Under the smoke, dust all over his mouth, laughing

with
    white teeth,
Under the terrible burden of destiny laughing as a young
    man laughs,
Laughing even as an ignorant fighter laughs who has
    never lost a battle,
Bragging and laughing that under his wrist is the pulse.
    and under his ribs the heart of the people,
        Laughing!
Laughing the stormy, husky, brawling laughter of
    Youth, half-naked, sweating, proud to be Hog
    Butcher, Tool Maker, Stacker of Wheat, Player with
    Railroads and Freight Handler to the Nation.

There are so many different worlds in Chicago. There are the edgier sections of Pilsen and Logan Square, the old city center in the Loop, the dramatic sweep of buildings along the Gold Coast fronting a beach that in summertime looks almost like it doesn't belong here, the Puerto Rican barrios of Humboldt Park and Devon Avenue, the elegant areas around Hyde Park, the craziness of Boystown, the world-class shopping along the Magnificent Mile, the theatre scene that's second only to what you'll find in New York, a music scene that's among the most vibrant in the country, you will find it almost impossible to absorb all this glorious city has to offer over a Long Weekend.

But you will get a taste so thrilling that you'll want to return again and again.

Chapter 2
GETTING ABOUT

It's easiest than you think to get around Chicago. One good thing about the practically totalitarian rule of the old mayor Richard Daley was that things got done and they got done fast. If a traffic light went out, it got fixed—and it got fixed NOW. That machinelike efficiency has declined somewhat with the passage of time and the lessening of control of the Mayor's Office, but the city is still remarkably well run for a major metro area.

CHICAGO TRANSIT AUTHORITY (CTA)
Customer Service: 312-836-7000
www.transitchicago.com
CTA runs buses and the famous elevated trains, a system efficiently serving not only the city, but some 35 or so suburban areas. Most routes run daily through late evening, every 10 to 20 minutes. Sundays and holidays have shortened schedules.

Routes are color-coded (Blue, Brown, Green, Orange, etc.), which makes it easy to find your way. In addition, there's an attendant on duty to assist you.

Various passes are available depending on how many passages you need to buy.

FROM O'HARE AIRPORT
Use the Blue line. Rapid transit trains to downtown Chicago get there in about 45 minutes. They depart from the CTA station inside the airport's Terminal3 (T3).

FROM MIDWAY AIRPORT
Use the Orange line.

CHICAGO OFFICE OF TOURISM
78 E Washington St (between Dearborn St & Michigan Ave), Chicago, 312-744-2400
www.ExploreChicago.org
NEIGHBORHOOD: The Loop

CHICAGO GREETER
77 E Randolph St (between Dearborn & Clark St), Chicago, 312-945-4231

www.chicagogreeter.com
NEIGHBORHOOD: The Loop
Discover the city with a greeter on a free informal visit to Chicago's sights. Pre-registration required.

CHICAGO NEIGHBORHOOD TOURS
77 E Randolph St (between Dearborn & Clark St), Chicago, 312-742-1190
NEIGHBORHOOD: The Loop
Tours leave from the Chicago Cultural Center. You get a feel for the city's many different communities from an insider's perspective with affordable half-day bus excursions celebrating the history, stories, traditions and people of Chicago. Reserve ahead.

Chapter 3
WHERE TO STAY

ACME HOTEL COMPANY
15 E Ohio St, Chicago, 312-894-0800
www.acmehotelcompany.com
NEIGHBORHOOD: Near North Side
This unique boutique hotel is ideal for those who appreciate design and a high-tech feel. This new hip hotel offers comfortable rooms filled with high-tech gadgets like Wi-Fi and smart TVs. Suites are wired for sound with Bowers and Wilkins Zeppelin wireless audio systems. Amenities include: free Wi-Fi, self-serve mini-bars, Lather bath products, free morning coffee, room service from West Town Bakery located in the lobby.

ALLEGRO CHICAGO, A KIMPTON HOTEL
171 W Randolph St (between Stetson Ave & Beaubien Ct), Chicago, 312-236-0123
www.allegrochicago.com

NEIGHBORHOOD: The Loop
A 483-room hotel in the city's bustling theater district, in the bold style of Kimpton hotels. Rooms from about $149.

BEST WESTERN HAWTHORN TERRACE
3434 N Broadway St, Chicago, 773-244-3434
www.hawthorneterrace.com
NEIGHBORHOOD: Lakeview
Located just steps away from the world-famous Wrigley Field, this lovely boutique hotel offers warm, stylish accommodations. Amenities include: free wireless high-speed Internet access, flat screen TVs, cable television, free bottled water and newspaper. Free breakfast. Conveniently located to local attractions, dining, and shopping.

CHICAGO ATHLETIC ASSOCIATION HOTEL
12 South Michigan Ave, Chicago, 312-940-3552
www.chicagoathletichotel.com
NEIGHBORHOOD: The Loop
Located in a restored Gothic-style building, this boutique hotel features industrial-chic guest rooms and suites. It was fashioned from an 1893 Venetian Gothic style building designed by Henry Ives Cobb, one of the most famous architects of the late 19th Century. The upgrade was designed by Roman & Williams, and it's really a spectacular job they've done. Amenities: complimentary Wi-Fi, flat-screen TVs, minibars, and marble bathrooms. Hotel features: rooftop restaurant, speakeasy-inspired game room/bar, burger joint and café. Conveniently located

within walking distance from Millennium Park and the Cloud Gate.

CITY SUITES HOTEL
933 W Belmont Ave, Chicago, 773-404-3400
www.chicagocitysuites.com
NEIGHBORHOOD: Lakeview
City Suites features Art Deco interiors with stylish, well-appointed suites and rooms. Amenities include: Free breakfast, free Wi-Fi, free gym access, free 24-hour coffee and afternoon cookies. Near attractions, nightlife, and the Belmont-Central Shopping District. No smoking in the property.

THE DRAKE
140 E Walton Place, Chicago, 312-787-2200
www.thedrakehotel.com
Writing about Chicago hotels without mentioning the Drake would be like writing about Denver without

mentioned the Brown Palace. When you are whisked into the lobby through one of the three golden revolving doors at the entrance, you realize you're in a special place. The hotel opened in 1920, and though it's been through a lot of change, it's still one of the grand hotels in Chicago. (Hilton bought it as long ago as 1980, but they've done well by it.) Even when I don't stay here, I slip into the **Coq d'Or** for a drink. If you have time, swing into the **Palm Court** for afternoon tea. Runs from 1 to 5. A harpist plucks strings in the background.

FREEHAND HOSTEL AND HOTEL
19 E Ohio St, Chicago, 312-940-3699
www.thefreehand.com/chicago
NEIGHBORHOOD: River North
Located in a classic 1927 building, Freehand Hotel offers unique hostel-style accommodations with both private and shared rooms. Amenities: Complimentary continental breakfast, complimentary Wi-Fi access, flat-screen TVs (select rooms), lockers and luggage storage. On-site restaurant – The Broken Shaker serves signature cocktails and small bites. Conveniently located within walking distance of the Magnificent Mile, shopping and local restaurants.

THE GODFREY HOTEL CHICAGO
127 West Huron at LaSalle Chicago, 312-649-2000
www.godfreyhotelchicago.com
NEIGHBORHOOD: North District
Industrial-chic luxury hotel offers 221 plush guest rooms and suites. Conveniently located within walking distance of the Magnificent Mile. It's also

close to the greatest concentration of art galleries, so this is a good place from which to explore the contemporary art scene in Chicago. The striking steel-and-glass structure has often been compared to a stack of Legos, and it's the first "staggered steel truss" building in town. (I'm not quite sure what that means, really, but it's still impressive visually.) Amenities: complimentary Wi-Fi, flat-screen TVs, and wet bars. Hotel features: spa, 24-hour fitness center, indoor/outdoor rooftop lounge (that happens to be the biggest one in town, with a retractable roof and 2-level fire pit), lobby restaurant and bar.

HAMPTON INN CHICAGO DOWNTOWN
68 East Wacker Place, Chicago, 312-419-9014
http://hamptoninn3.hilton.com
NEIGHBORHOOD: Downtown - Loop
Located in a landmark Chicago building, this hotel features beautiful guest rooms and suites. The multi-storied lobby has been meticulously restored. Look next door and you'll see the stunning art Deco Chicago Motor Club building, a wonderful architectural landmark. Amenities: Complimentary breakfast, complimentary Wi-Fi, flat-screen TVs, and mini-fridges. Hotel features: lobby bar and 24-hour fitness center. Conveniently located near Magnificent Mile and the Chicago Riverwalk.

HOTEL LINCOLN
1816 N Clark St, Chicago, 312-254-4700
www.jdvhotels.com
NEIGHBORHOOD: Lincoln Park

Overlooking Lincoln Park, the Lincoln (in an historic inn dating from the 1920s) is a contemporary 184-room hotel decorated with both modern and vintage details. Many of the rooms have scenic views of Lake Michigan. Amenities include: Free Wi-Fi, 24-hour Fitness center, iPod/iPad docking stations, rooftop yoga, and free bike rentals, Flat-screen LCD TVs, and free wine hour. Two on-site restaurants and a rooftop bar that I really love in the summer. Pet friendly. Near Wrigley Field and other cultural attractions like Second City.

THE HOXTON CHICAGO
200 N Green St, 312-761-1700
www.thehoxton.com
NEIGHBORHOOD: Fulton Market District
Former industrial space transformed into a 182-room luxury hotel featuring warehouse-style floor-to-ceiling windows. Three size rooms – Snug, Cosy and Roomy. Amenities: Rooftop pool, fitness studio, and complimentary high-speed Internet. Three bars and restaurants on-site. Pet friendly. Located in the busy Fulton Market District near galleries, boutiques, and some of the city's best bars and restaurants.

HYATT PLACE CHICAGO/DOWNTOWN
28 North Franklin St Chicago, 312-955-0950
www.hyatt.com/en-US/hotel/illinois/hyatt-place-chicago-downtown-the-loop/chizp
NEIGHBORHOOD: The Loop
Modern 8-story building featuring over 200 guest rooms near the Financial and Theatre Districts. Amenities: complimentary Wi-Fi, flat-screen TVs,

wet bars, mini-fridges, and iPod docks.
Complimentary hot breakfast. Hotel features: 24-hour snack bar, mini-mart, café/bar, indoor pool, and 24-hour fitness room. Conveniently located near shopping and local cultural centers.

THE LANGHAM
330 N Wabash Ave, Chicago, 312-923-9988
www.langhamhotels.com
NEIGHBORHOOD: Near North Side
Set in a Mies van der Rohe landmark tower designed in 1971 as the IBM Tower and overlooking the Chicago River, this hotel features 316 luxury guest rooms. The lobby and other public rooms are worthy your attention, if only because you feel like you're being transported back into the mid-20th Century. Amenities: 55-inch flat-screen TVs, iPod docking stations, complimentary Wi-Fi and coffee makers. On-site day spa, restaurant, lounge, health club and spa.

LOEWS CHICAGO HOTEL
455 North Park Drive Chicago, 312-840-6600
www.loewshotels.com/Chicago
NEIGHBORHOOD: Downtown
A sophisticated high-rise featuring 400 guest rooms and suites perched on the north bank of the Chicago River which you can see through the floor-to-ceiling windows installed in the rooms here. Relaxing color scheme of gray and ivory tones. Amenities: complimentary Wi-Fi, flat-screen Smart TVs, coffeemakers, and iPod docks. Hotel features: fitness center, 75-foot indoor lap pool, and spa. Close to Millennium Park and Navy Pier.

MAJESTIC HOTEL
528 W Brompton Ave, Chicago, 773-404-3499
www.majestic-chicago.com
NEIGHBORHOOD: Lakeview
This boutique hotel has a cozy fire burning in the lobby and an English influenced décor. 52 rooms and suites. Amenities include: Free breakfast, free Wi-Fi, free gym access, and free afternoon cookies. Near Wrigley Field and other attractions, shopping and dining. No smoking.

PARK HYATT CHICAGO
800 N Michigan Ave, Chicago, 312-335-1234
https://chicago.park.hyatt.com/en/hotel/home.html
NEIGHBORHOOD: Downtown/Near North Side
This hotel offers luxury accommodations in an atmosphere of contemporary chic. There's a cool rooftop deck on the seventh floor where you can have

lunch. The hotel features 198 guestrooms and suites elegantly understated with amenities like: free Wi-Fi. Three on-site restaurants, a cocktail lounge and a chocolate bar. Indoor pool and spa.

RENAISSANCE BLACKSTONE
636 S Michigan Ave, 312-447-0955
www.marriott.com
NEIGHBORHOOD: South Loop
Across from Grant Park, this gorgeous hotel is set in a beautiful 1910 Beaux Arts building, this ornate hotel offers 335 guestrooms and suites. When the place went through a restoration in 2008, they found gilded walnut paneling and brass bannisters that had been covered up for decades. Every president from William Taft to Jimmy Carter has stayed here. (I don't blame them!) Amenities: Wi-Fi (fee), flat-screen TVs, iPod docks and mini-fridges. Hotel features: Contemporary Spanish restaurant, coffee shop, 24-hour exercise room, and a commissioned collection of more than 1,600 art works on view in the public areas. Pet-friendly rooms. Conveniently located near the Field Museum and just a mile from Willis Tower.

SOHO HOUSE CHICAGO
113-125 N Green St, Chicago, 312-521-8000
www.sohohousechicago.com
NEIGHBORHOOD: Near West Side, West Loop
Refined 40-room hotel featuring a posh members-only club (and one of the few Soho House locations open to the public). It's worth staying here just to get the view of the skyline from the rooftop here. While

the restaurants are open to the public, the rooftop is reserved for club members and hotel guests. Amenities: Complimentary Wi-Fi and smoke free rooms. Hotel features: 60-foot rooftop pool, fitness center, club bar, two public restaurants, and music room. The 17,000 square-foot gym and professional boxing ring are accessible to members and hotel guests.

THOMPSON CHICAGO
21 E Bellevue Pl, Chicago, 312-266-2100
www.thompsonhotels.com
NEIGHBORHOOD: Gold Coast
Located in the heart of Chicago, this Thompson Hotel offers luxurious accommodations and sophisticated guest services. The hotel offers 247 guestrooms and suites, including six duplex loft suites with private terraces offering stunning views not only of the lake but the city as well. Decorated with the sophisticated look inspired by vintage collections of Yves Saint Laurent, this hotel promises guests a luxury stay. Lots of shiny leather, lots of velvet, lots of burnished dark woods. Opulent wouldn't be a bad word to use when describing this place. The hotel features two on-site restaurants: **Nico Osteria** and **Salone Nico**. Conveniently located near Michigan Avenue, shopping, restaurants and nightlife. On-site 1,000-square foot fitness center. Pets are welcome, too, and not just little ones, but any size. (I wouldn't bring my pet giraffe, however.)

VIRGIN HOTEL CHICAGO
203 North Wabash, Chicago, 312-940-4400

https://virginhotels.com/
NEIGHBORHOOD: The Loop
Richard Branson has slapped the Virgin logo on everything from record stores to airplanes. Now it's hotels. This ultramodern hotel features 250 guest rooms and suites, but there's so much going on in this hip hotel property that you won't want to waste much time in your room. The lobby gets packed at 5 p.m. as people converge at the wine bar. On the second floor, there's the **Commons Club** and the **Shag Room**. The rooftop terrace is packed in good weather, and filled with people that look more beautiful than I do. When it all gets to be too much, you can retreat to the spa in the basement with its 5 treatment rooms and a hammam. Amenities: complimentary Wi-Fi, flat-screen TVs, minibars, rainfall showers, and 24-hour room service. Hotel facilities: modern American diner, rooftop bar, coffee shop, 24-hour fitness center, and spa. 5 unique restaurant and lounge experiences. Conveniently located near shopping, restaurants, and entertainment venues.

WALDORF ASTORIA CHICAGO
11 E Walton St (bet. State St & Rush Sts), Chicago, 312-646-1300
www.waldorfastoria3.hilton.com
NEIGHBORHOOD: Near North Side
It is a cushy 188-room hotel where the beds are adorned with 460-thread-count Rivolta Carmignani linens. From the outside, the building, not far from the Magnificent Mile, resembles a chateau. Rooms start at over $400.

THE WILLOWS HOTEL
555 W Surf St, Chicago, 773-528-8400
www.willowshotelchicago.com
This premium hotel offers the charm of a French country home with great service. Amenities include: Free breakfast, free Wi-Fi, free gym access, free afternoon cookies, free coffee 24-hours, and hosted evening happy hour. Just two blocks from Lake Michigan, this is another smoke-free hotel.

Chapter 4
WHERE TO EAT

ALINEA
1723 N Halsted St, 312-867-0110
www.alinearestaurant.com
CUISINE: American (New)/European
DRINKS: Wine
SERVING: Dinner
PRICE RANGE: $$$$
NEIGHBORHOOD: Lincoln Park
Foodies love this small two-level eatery with each floor offering a different dining experience. The atmosphere is not 'fun,' but severely elegant in a most restrained way. You might even call it austere. (I've had more fun in church, sad to say.) If you don't take food as seriously as they do, stay away. Unique

dishes are more like art creations, menu changes often. "The Kitchen Table" gets you into a room with just the chef & waiters. 6 people only. Expensive. Then there are 2 prix-fixe menus, the "Gallery" with 16-to-18 courses served on the ground floor, and the "Salon" menu, served upstairs, which has 10-12 courses. Check current (very high) prices, and plan on spending the whole evening there. Favorites: Wagyu beef and Asian street food. Excellent wine pairings.

ANN SATHER
909 W Belmont Ave, Chicago, 773-348-2378
www.annsather.com
CUISINE: Scandinavian
DRINKS: No Booze
SERVING: Breakfast, Brunch
PRICE RANGE: $$
NEIGHBORHOOD: Lakeview
One of several scattered throughout Chicago, this Swedish eatery serves up one of the best breakfasts in town. Menu favorites include: Swedish Breakfast and once you taste one of their fresh-baked cinnamon rolls, you'll rave about them too.

ARBOR
2545 W Diversey Ave, Chicago, 312-866-0795
www.arborprojects.com
CUISINE: American (New)
DRINKS: Full Bar
SERVING: Breakfast & Lunch; closed Sat & Sun
PRICE RANGE: $$
NEIGHBORHOOD: Logan Square

Industrial kitchen and coffeehouse serving breakfast & lunch only. Menu picks: Breakfast burrito and Rhubarb oatmeal. Wine pairings and crafted cocktails. Daily specials.

ARCADIA
1639 S Wabash Ave, Chicago, 312-360-9500
www.acadiachicago.com
CUISINE: American
DRINKS: Full Bar
SERVING: Dinner
PRICE RANGE: $$$$
NEIGHBORHOOD: Near Southside/South Loop
Run by Chef Ryan McCaskey, this high-end eatery offers a creative menu featuring dishes like Lobster potpie and Black cod. If you're a meat lover, try the Wagu tri-tip, a meat and potatoes dish with thick slices of beef. Desserts are just as interesting and

delicious especially the chocolate pudding that's filled with pieces of sponge cake, hazelnuts, and almond-cookie shards. The bar serves novel cocktails and offers a nice wine list. The décor is simple but comfortable. Closed Monday and Tuesday.

ARTOPOLIS BAKERY & CAFE
306 S Halsted St, Chicago, 312-559-9000
www.artopolischicago.com
CUISINE: Greek
DRINKS: Full Bar
SERVING: Brunch, Lunch, Dinner
PRICE RANGE: $$
NEIGHBORHOOD: Near West Side
A combination bakery, café, bar and retail shop. Here you'll find fresh baked Greek pastries like their signature "artopitas." Their menu features a selection of soups, salads, wood-fired pizzas and sandwiches made with hearth-baked bread. Traditional Greek dishes like eggplant moussaka and roasted leg of lamb are also offered. In the shop you'll find breads and pastries, gift baskets, chocolates, olive oils and vinegars.

ATWOOD CAFÉ
1 W Washington St, Chicago, 312-368-1900
www.atwoodrestaurant.com
CUISINE: American
DRINKS: Full Bar
SERVING: Breakfast, Lunch, Dinner
PRICE RANGE: $$$
NEIGHBORHOOD: The Loop
Located in the historic Reliance Building along with the **Hotel Burnham**, this restaurant offers classic American cuisine served in an Art Deco decorated dining room that features 18-foot-tall windows. Chef Derek Simcik's menu features dishes made with fresh, seasonal ingredients. Menu favorites include: Roasted chicken and Vegetable pot pie. Great choice for pre-theater nosh.

AU CHEVAL
800 W Randolph St, Chicago, 312-929-4580
www.auchevalchicago.com
CUISINE: American (New)
DRINKS: Full Bar

SERVING: Lunch, Dinner
PRICE RANGE: $$
NEIGHBORHOOD: West Loop
Upscale diner-style eatery with an open kitchen. Great varied menu but they are famous for their burgers. Menu picks: Honey-fried chicken and Cheeseburger. Usually a wait since there's limited seating.

AVEC
615 W Randolph St, Chicago, 312-377-2002
www.avecrestaurant.com
CUISINE: French/Mediterranean
DRINKS: Full Bar
SERVING: Lunch & Dinner
PRICE RANGE: $$$
NEIGHBORHOOD: Near West Side
This intimate restaurant offers a small plate menu and communal seating. Menu favorites include Ricotta flatbread, Pork shoulder and Papperdelle. No reservations – which means there's often a wait. Now serving brunch.

BAD HUNTER
802 W Randolph St, Chicago, 312-265-1745
www.badhunter.com
CUISINE: American (New)
DRINKS: Full bar
SERVING: Lunch & Dinner
PRICE RANGE: $$
NEIGHBORHOOD: Near West Side, West Loop
Hip restaurant with a vegetable-focused menu. Favorites: Smoked salmon tartine and Butternut

Squash sandwich. Bar serves low-alcohol craft cocktails.

BAKERY AT FAT RICE
2951 W Diversey Ave, Chicago, 773-661-9544
www.eatfatrice.com
CUISINE: Bakery
DRINKS: No Booze
SERVING: Breakfast, Lunch; closed Mon & Tues
PRICE RANGE: $$
NEIGHBORHOOD: Logan Square
Eclectic bakery that also serves breakfast & lunch. Portuguese-style sweet dough has baked into it Vienna all-beef hot dog, hot sport peppers, chopped onion, tomato and then topped with poppy & celery seeds and spread with Chinese mustard. Wow. There's a great Char siu pineapple bun filled with BBQ pork.

BERGHOFF
17 W Adams St, Chicago, 312-427-3170
www.theberghoff.com
CUISINE: German

DRINKS: Full Bar
SERVING: Lunch, Dinner
PRICE RANGE: $$
NEIGHBORHOOD: The Loop
A Chicago landmark, this restaurant serves German-style cuisine offering a variety of appetizers, salads, sandwiches, and entrees including vegetarian and gluten-free dishes. But gluten-free is not what you come here for. It's that big juicy Reuben on rye that is hard to hold in two hands. Menu favorites include: Weiner Schnitzel and Jagerschnitzel - Pork Cutlet, with mushrooms and bacon. Good selection of German beer and lagers.

BIG JONES
5347 N Clark St, 773-275-5725
www.bigjoneschicago.com
CUISINE: Southern
DRINKS: Full Bar
SERVING: Lunch & Dinner, Weekend Brunch
PRICE RANGE: $$
NEIGHBORHOOD: Andersonville
Modern style eatery with a nice little bar area up front before it turns into a long narrow room with tables on either side. Very simple but comfortable. There's a fenced-in patio out back that's nice in good weather. Serves Southern-style cooking from New Orleans and the Carolina Lowcountry. Favorites: Cajun Boudin Balls (breaded liver sausage); Rutabaga Bisque (I know, but trust me—it's delicious); Crispy Catfish (with a unique corn and rice flour breading I hadn't seen in many years); Gumbo Ya-Ya (very strong Cajun elements—very nice) and Barbecued Pork

Shoulder (smoked with pecan wood). The fried chicken is also very highly recommended—they cook it in lard and ham drippings. (Bring a Lipitor!) Back patio available weather permitting.

BIG STAR
1531 N Damen, (bet. Wicker Park Ave & Pierce Ave), Chicago, 773-235-4039
www.bigstarchicago.com
CUISINE: Mexican, Tex-Mex
DRINKS: Full Bar
SERVING: Lunch, Dinner & Late Night
PRICE RANGE: $$
NEIGHBORHOOD: Wicker Park
Nice range of Mexican food, from fish, chicken and beef tacos, to a Sonoran Hot Dag (a bacon-wrapped hot dog with pinto beans, lime mayo, mustard, onions and Big Star hot sauce on a bolillo roll). Most people don't know it, but Big Star has blended 20+ signature barrels of whiskey with some of Kentucky's best distilleries, creating perhaps the biggest single-barrel selection in the U.S. If you like American whiskey, you MUST put a stop here at the top of your list.

BILLY GOAT TAVERN
430 N Michigan Ave (Lower Level), Chicago, 312-222-1525
www.billygoattavern.com
CUISINE: American, Burgers
DRINKS: Full Bar
SERVING: Lunch & Dinner
PRICE RANGE: $
NEIGHBORHOOD: Near North Side
Located underneath the Chicago Tribune Building, this tavern offers a genuine diner/soda fountain feel. Worth a stop if you're in the neighborhood but other than that the burgers aren't that impressive. Locations all over the city.

BLACKBIRD
619 W Randolph St, Chicago, 312-715-0708
www.blackbirdrestaurant.com
CUISINE: American
DRINKS: Full Bar
SERVING: Lunch & Dinner
PRICE RANGE: $$$

NEIGHBORHOOD: Near West Side
They can claim Michelin stars here since 2011, and the cooks here (sorry, chefs) have more James Beard Awards than you can shake a stick at. I find the décor to be antiseptic and clinically sleek and modern, to the point that the bar looks like a big white slab on which a medical examiner might conduct an autopsy. It's about as warm and fuzzy and charming in here as a meat locker. But if you look past the studied modernity of the setting, you'll love the food: roasted chicken roulade, hanger steak with rutabaga (I love rutabaga, and you so seldom see it offered), wood-grilled sturgeon with roasted leeks, sucking pig served with risotto (dinner only), poached turbot (the most delicate I've had in a long time), and the aged duck breast, simply outstanding.

CAFÉ MARIE- JEANNE
1001 N California Ave, Chicago,773-904-7660
www.cafe-marie-jeanne.com
CUISINE: French
DRINKS: Full Bar
SERVING: Breakfast, Lunch, & Dinner; closed Tues
PRICE RANGE: $$
NEIGHBORHOOD: West Town, Humboldt Park
Cozy French café with a deli counter. Menu is a la cart. One favorite is their Avocado toast with raspberry vinaigrette jam. Or the bursting-with-flavor duck frites. Or the calf brains served on brioche toast. Great selection of wines, craft beers and liquors. Top-notch brunch.

CELLAR DOOR PROVISIONS
3025 W Diversey Ave, Chicago, 773-697-8337
www.cellardoorprovisions.com
CUISINE: American (New)
DRINKS: Full Bar
SERVING: Breakfast, Lunch (till 3) Wed-Sun;
Dinner till 9 on Fri-Sat; Closed Mon & Tues
PRICE RANGE: $$
NEIGHBORHOOD: Logan Square
Low-key neighborhood eatery offering a simple but exquisitely prepared menu. They have the best bread in town, with croissants that have a flakiness that will surprise and please you. Decadent quiche. The ashwood chairs and Spartan tables are about as basic as you can get, but that doesn't matter. Light streams in from the high windows on the street. While it's a perfect place for breakfast or lunch, on the 2 nights they served their very reasonably priced prix fixe dinner, you get a four-course meal you won't soon forget. Items like corn soup, plum salad, roasted peaches. Nice choice for brunch. Lots of vegetable-focused dishes with international ingredients.

CESAR'S RESTAURANT
3166 N Clark St, Chicago, 773-248-2835
www.killermargaritas.com/eat.html
CUISINE: Mexican
DRINKS: Full Bar
SERVING: Dinner
PRICE RANGE: $$
NEIGHBORHOOD: Lakeview
This Mexican restaurant serves delicious authentic Mexican fare and is known for its lip-smacking

margaritas. Check out their website for special events like Cinco de Mayo and Pride Parade. Good food and friendly service. (Try the Peach margaritas.)

THE CHICAGO CHOP HOUSE
60 W Ontario St, Chicago, 312-787-7100
www.chicagochophouse.com
CUISINE: Steakhouse
DRINKS: Full Bar
SERVING: Dinner
PRICE RANGE: $$$$
NEIGHBORHOOD: Near North Side
Located in a century-old Victorian, this place serves Mishima Ranch Wagyu Beef and is one of the best steakhouses in the city. Menu includes their famous 64-ounce porterhouse steak with a pretty good list of wines by the glass. Portraits of old Chicago gangsters (lots of those to choose from, including a few politicians) hang on the wall and the clientele is filled with regulars who are serious about their steaks.

THE CHICAGO DINER
3411 N Halsted St, Chicago, 773-935-6696
www.veggiediner.com
CUISINE: Vegetarian, Vegan
DRINKS: Beer & Wine Only
SERVING: Lunch, Dinner
PRICE RANGE: $$
NEIGHBORHOOD: Lakeview
A landmark vegetarian/vegan diner that has been serving good food for more than 20 years. Comfort food with a vegetarian twist. Menu favorites include: Portobello mushroom burgers and a Nacho appetizer. Yummy desserts. Even if you think you hate vegan food, give this place a try. As Lucille Ball said about Vitameatavegamin in that famous commercial, "It's so tasty, too!"

COALFIRE PIZZA
1321 W Grand Ave, Chicago, 312-226-2625
www.coalfirechicago.com
CUISINE: Pizza
DRINKS: Beer & Wine
SERVING: Lunch, Dinner
PRICE RANGE: $$
NEIGHBORHOOD: Near West Side
Here you'll find an American version of the traditional Neapolitan style pizza made in an 800-degree clean burning coal oven.

CITY MOUSE
Ace Hotel
311 N Morgan St, Chicago, 312-764-1908
www.citymousechicago.com
CUISINE: American (New)
DRINKS: Full Bar
SERVING: Breakfast, Lunch, & Dinner
PRICE RANGE: $$
NEIGHBORHOOD: Fulton Market, West Loop, Near West Side
Comfortable eatery offering a menu of New American fare. One favorite is their goat cheese gnudi with braised lamb shank. Or the green curry with butternut squash and king crab. Or Chinese broccoli with roasted San Marzano tomatoes. A lot of the veggies served here are grown in the Ace Hotel's garden operated by Roof Crop. Daily brunch is served. Craft cocktails. Gluten-free options.

CORRIDOR BREWERY & PROVISIONS
3446 N Southport, Chicago, 773-270-4272

www.corridorchicago.com
CUISINE: American (New)
DRINKS: Full Bar
SERVING: Lunch & Dinner
PRICE RANGE: $$
NEIGHBORHOOD: Lakeview
Located in the center of the Southport Corridor, this Farmhouse craft brewery and restaurant offers a menu of Midwestern favorites like sandwiches and artisan pizzas. Beers available only in the brewery.

DRYHOP BREWERS
3155 N Broadway St, Chicago, 773-857-3155
www.dryhopchicago.com
CUISINE: American (New)
DRINKS: Full Bar
SERVING: Lunch & Dinner
PRICE RANGE: $$
NEIGHBORHOOD: Lakeview
Combination brewery and kitchen with a focus on the brews. Menu features simple shared plates of comfort food. Menu picks: Fried chicken sandwich and mac n cheese. New beer selections weekly.

DUSEK'S
1227 W 18th St, Chicago, 312-526-3851
www.dusekschicago.com
CUISINE: American
DRINKS: Full Bar
SERVING: Dinner
PRICE RANGE: $$
NEIGHBORHOOD: Pilsen

More than a bar, this place has become a popular eatery. Menu favorites include: Boneless Duck wings, Red Snapper Crudo, and Juicy Lucy burger. A dessert favorite is the chocolate bar, served with a knife and fork as it's served on a bed of marshmallow fluff and caramel drizzle. When you leave visit the Punch Bar downstairs for one of their specialty punches.

ELSKE
1350 W Randolph St, Chicago, 312-733-1314
www.elskerestaurant.com
CUISINE: American (New)

DRINKS: Full Bar
SERVING: Dinner; closed Mon & Tues
PRICE RANGE: $$$$
NEIGHBORHOOD: Near West Side, West Loop
Comfortable eatery with an affordable tasting menu. Enjoy cocktails by the fireplace outside. Prix fixe menu with wine pairings is quite popular. Favorites: Confit maitakes with creamed barley and Fermented black bean agnolotti with morels. The sweets on offer here are particularly delectable.

FAT RICE
2957 W Diversey Ave, Chicago, 773-661-9170
www.eatfatrice.com
CUISINE: Asian Fusion/Chinese
DRINKS: Full Bar
SERVING: Lunch & Dinner; Lunch only on Sun; Closed Mon
PRICE RANGE: $$
NEIGHBORHOOD: Logan Square
Rustic style eatery where you eat on communal tables with an open kitchen. The place is decorated with items picked up on trips the owners have made to far-flung locales, very nice, comfortable and homey. The cuisine here emphasis dishes from the Macau area (those of you good with geography will know that Macau was once a Portuguese colony). Besides the Macanese food, the menu features Asian inspired comfort food and also some Portuguese dishes. Menu picks: Sichuan-style bacon (with bacon they smoke in-house, wood ear mushrooms and 5-spice powder), Pork Chop Bun and Piri-Piri Chicken, Sichuan eggplant pickles; Potstickers; arroz gordo (fat rice)

with salted duck, roast pork, littleneck clams, and Portuguese chicken.

FLORIOLE CAFÉ & BAKERY
1220 W Webster Ave, Chicago, 773-883-1313
www.floriole.com
CUISINE: Bakery/Cafe
DRINKS: No Booze
SERVING: Breakfast/Lunch
PRICE RANGE: $$
NEIGHBORHOOD: Lincoln Park
Bakery and café serving a variety of fresh pastries. The upstairs dining room is particularly nice when the weather is clean and the sun bursts through the windows. Small menu of soups, salads, and quiches. Friday night is Pizza Night. Of course the coffee's great.

FRONTERA GRILL
445 N Clark St, Chicago, 312-661-1434
www.fronterakitchens.com
CUISINE: Mexican

DRINKS: Full Bar
SERVING: Lunch, Dinner
PRICE RANGE: $$$
NEIGHBORHOOD: Near North Side
Open since 1987, the popularity of this Mexican grill can probably be credited to Celebrity Chef and winner of Top Chef Masters Rick Bayless. The ever-changing menu features Mexican classics like enchiladas, mole and flautas. Menu favorites include: Oyster & Ceviche Combo and Carne Asada (Rib steak, bean and sweet plantain with a little bit of guac).

GALIT
2429 N Lincoln Ave, 773-360-8755
www.galitrestaurant.com
CUISINE: Middle Eastern/Mediterranean/Vegetarian
DRINKS: Full Bar
SERVING: Dinner, Closed Mondays
PRICE RANGE: $$
NEIGHBORHOOD: Lincoln Park
Hip Middle Eastern eatery with a few kitchen-side seats if you want to watch while the cooks do their thing. Otherwise, tables against the walls provide more privacy. Offering regular & shared menus. Favorites: Brisket Hummus (among several you can choose from); Carrots grilled are very flavorful, as are all of the veggie choices here; Falafel (mango, labneh, pickled turnips); Beets with black garlic; Chick thigh with crispy skin (this is really good); Balkan Stuffed Cabbage with lamb kebab. As a rule, you don't often see "creative cocktails" in a place serving this kind of food, so this is a plus. Reservations recommended.

GIANT
3209 W Armitage Ave, Chicago, 773-252-0997
www.giantrestaurant.com
CUISINE: American (New)
DRINKS: Full bar
SERVING: Dinner; closed Sun & Mon
PRICE RANGE: $$$
NEIGHBORHOOD: Logan Square
Funky restaurant set in an art decorated storefront gets its name from "Me and My Giant," a poem by Shel Silverstein who was originally from Logan Square. Cozy and casual eatery with a menu of shared dishes. The chef here takes comfort food and elevates it to something really special and unexpected. Imagine onion rings, but fried in Parmesan batter, or sweet corn fancied up with peanuts, mint and Thai chiles. Favorites: Garlic buttermilk potatoes, Happy Scallops, Chicken habanero and Sweet & sour eggplant (excellent dish you must try). Great wine selection.

GIBSONS BAR & STEAKHOUSE
1028 N Rush St (bet. Cedar St & Oak St), Chicago
312-266-8999
www.gibsonssteakhouse.com
CUISINE: Steakhouse
DRINKS: Full Bar
SERVING: Lunch, Dinner
PRICE RANGE: $$$
NEIGHBORHOOD: Near North Side
This is a very popular restaurant with traditional menu offerings of steaks, chops and seafood. The

delicious desserts are bountiful. It's busy, so book ahead.

GILT BAR
230 W Kinzie St, Chicago, 312-464-9544
www.giltbarchicago.com
CUISINE: American
DRINKS: Full Bar
SERVING: Dinner
PRICE RANGE: $$$
NEIGHBORHOOD: Near North Side, River North
Credit the recession, but a number of good mid-price but high-style restaurants have opened in Chicago in the last two years. A favorite is "Gilt Bar," a casual restaurant in the River North neighborhood that isn't casual about its cooking. The menu features New American dishes like blackened cauliflower with capers ($7) and ricotta gnocchi with sage and brown butter ($13). After dinner, head downstairs to Curio, a basement bar with a Prohibition theme. Try the

Death's Door Daisy, made with artisanal Wisconsin vodka and Aperol, a blood orange liqueur, for $10.

GIRL & THE GOAT
809 W Randolph St (bet. Green & Halsted Sts), Chicago, 312-492-6262
www.girlandthegoat.com
CUISINE: American
DRINKS: Full Bar
SERVING: Dinner
PRICE RANGE: $$$
NEIGHBORHOOD: Near West Side, West Loop
A much-blogged-about new restaurant where the "Top Chef" winner Stephanie Izard takes livestock parts seriously. The often-updated menu recently included lamb ribs with grilled avocado and pistachio piccata ($17), and braised beef tongue with masa and beef vinaigrette ($12). If you're not a carnivore, try chickpeas three ways ($11), and for dessert, potato fritters with lemon poached eggplant and Greek yogurt ($8). The soaring dining room, designed by the Chicago design firm 555 International, is warm and modern, with exposed beams, walls of charred cedar and a large open kitchen.

GOOD FORTUNE
2528 N California Ave, 773-666-5238
www.goodfortunechicago.com
CUISINE: American (New)/Mediterranean
DRINKS: Full Bar
SERVING: Dinner, Closed Mon & Tues.
PRICE RANGE: $$
NEIGHBORHOOD: Logan Square

Popular eatery in a narrow room with a bar on one side and tables on the other. Dim lighting at night creates a fun, intimate atmosphere, but it's still quite lively, not romantic and quiet. A wood-burning oven is used to prepare a lot of their dishes, and they know how to use it effectively. The menu is a bit all over the place, so you might get a Mediterranean dish followed by one from the Midwest. Favorites: Marinated beets (with fennel); Black Garlic Rigatoni; Prawns with head on served with octopus & black lentils; Roasted pork collar (from that wood-burning oven I mentioned); and a superior Ribeye with whipped celery root & bone marrow. Creative desserts and cocktails.

GT FISH & OYSTER
531 N Wells St, Chicago, 312-929-3501
www.gtoyster.com
CUISINE: Seafood / Creole / Cajun
DRINKS: Full Bar

SERVING: Lunch, Dinner
PRICE RANGE: $$$
NEIGHBORHOOD: Near North Side
This popular Cajun style seafood eatery offers an impressive small plates seasonal menu featuring a variety of fresh oysters, crab cakes, lobster rolls and calamari. Menu favorites include: Tuna pokem Oyster Po-Boy and Shrimp bruschetta. Impressive beer & wine menu.

HONKY TONK BARBEQUE
1800 S Racine Ave, Chicago, 312-226-7427
www.honkytonkbbqchicago.com
CUISINE: Barbeque
DRINKS: Full Bar
SERVING: Dinner
PRICE RANGE: $$
NEIGHBORHOOD: Pilsen
Popular hangout offering a full schedule of live music that covers the genres of American Roots music including: roaring 20s, groovy 60s; Western Swing, Honky Tonk, Rockabilly, Bluegrass, Blues, Old Time, Soul, and occasionally new age indie and rock. Menu features Championship BBQ pork, beef, chicken and other made-from-scratch dishes. This is a late night bar with theme nights like Trivia night on Wednesdays.

JAM
2853 N Kedzie Ave, Chicago, 773-292-6011
www.jamrestaurant.com
CUISINE: Breakfast, Brunch
DRINKS: Full Bar

SERVING: Breakfast, Brunch
PRICE RANGE: $$
NEIGHBORHOOD: Logan Square
While this restaurant serves both breakfast and lunch, it has earned a reputation as one of the nation's most celebrated brunch restaurants. Chef Jeffrey Mauro offers a creative menu featuring favorites like: the egg sandwich, the burrito suizo, and malted French toast.

LA SERENA CLANDESTINA
954 W Fulton Market, Chicago, 312-226-5300
www.lasirenachicago.com
CUISINE: Latin American/Brazilian
DRINKS: Full Bar
SERVING: Lunch, Dinner; closed for lunch on Sat
PRICE RANGE: $$
NEIGHBORHOOD: Fulton Market, West Loop
Cute little dining spot with a farmhouse feel. Simple menu filled with shared plate items. The standout here is the exquisite ceviche. Nice selection of wines.

LES NOMADES
222 E Ontario St, Chicago, 312-649-9010
www.lesnomades.net
CUISINE: French
DRINKS: Full Bar
SERVING: Dinner; closed Sun & Mon
PRICE RANGE: $$$$
NEIGHBORHOOD: River East
Upscale eatery located in a brownstone that throws off a lot of charm is this place that offers "French haute cuisine" and an impressive wine list (with lots of Champagnes). Menu picks: Warm lobster and

shrimp salad and Langoustine ravioli with sea scallop. For dessert they offer a variety of exceptional soufflés. Great ambiance for a romantic date.

LITTLE GOAT BREAD
820 W Randolph St, Chicago, 312-888-3455
www.littlegoatchicago.com
CUISINE: American/Bakery
DRINKS: Full Bar
SERVING: Breakfast, Lunch, Dinner
PRICE RANGE: $$
NEIGHBORHOOD: Near West Side
Celebrated Chef Stephanie Izard offers a simple menu of American favorites in this updated version of a diner with things like Shrimp & Grits and Bull's Eye French Toast. Comfortable diner-like atmosphere.

LONGMAN & EAGLE
2657 N Kedzie Ave, (bet. Milwaukee & Schubert Aves), Chicago, 773-276-7110
www.longmanandeagle.com
CUISINE: American
DRINKS: Full Bar
SERVING: Breakfast, Lunch & Dinner
PRICE RANGE: $$
NEIGHBORHOOD: Logan Square
It is a rough-edged bar that serves a refined brunch: a chunky sockeye salmon tartare with pickled mango ($10) or a wild boar "Sloppy Joe" ($10). Six hotel rooms upstairs. Logan Square, about five to six miles northwest of the Loop, is a remnant of Chicago's late-19th-century beautification movement, with a statue

of an eagle by Evelyn Longman where two of the grandest boulevards meet.

MAUDE'S LIQUOR BAR
840 W Randolph St, Chicago, 312-243-9712
www.maudesliquorbar.com
CUISINE: French
DRINKS: Full Bar
SERVING: Dinner
PRICE RANGE: $$$
NEIGHBORHOOD: Near West Side
Run by **Au Cheval** owner Brendan Sodikoff, Maude's is certainly more than a liquor bar. On the first floor there's a dining room with a marble bar and on the second there's a sunken, plush bar. Heavy on atmosphere (dimly lit with candles / exposed brick) with a nice French menu of seafood and classic

dishes. Very romantic feeling about the place. The excellent classic cocktails only enhance the experience. Menu picks: Steak tartare, Mussels, and French Onion fondue, Escargot and Gnocchi.

MI TOCAYA ANTOJERIA
2800 W Logan Blvd, Chicago, 872-315-3947
www.mitocaya.com
CUISINE: Mexican/Latin American
DRINKS: Full Bar
SERVING: Dinner; closed Mon
PRICE RANGE: $$
NEIGHBORHOOD: Logan Square
Relaxed eatery offering a menu of Mexican small plates. Favorites: Peanut butter lengua and Duck leg (carnitas style). Crispy sweetbreads are served with gremolata. Mussels come with cabbage and radishes. The steak burrito oozes with melted cheese and salty beef. Patio dining – weather permitting. Nice selection of desserts and cocktails.

MIA FRANCESCA
3311 N Clark St, Chicago, 773-281-3310
www.miafrancesca.com
CUISINE: Italian
DRINKS: Full Bar
SERVING: Dinner
PRICE RANGE: $$
NEIGHBORHOOD: Lakeview
Popular chain restaurant in these parts serving solid if not terribly imaginative Italian fare. Noisy and crowded. Menu favorites include: Rigatoni con scarola and chicken salvia. Outdoor patio.

MOMOTARO
820 W Lake St, Chicago, 312-733-4818
www.momotarochicago.com
CUISINE: Sushi
DRINKS: Full bar
SERVING: Dinner
PRICE RANGE: $$$

NEIGHBORHOOD: Fulton Market, Near West Side, West Loop

This $3.4 million, 11,000-square-foot two-level venue is impressive in size, decoration and its giant menu (and I really mean a giant menu—it's vast). Sushi fans flock to this spot. On the ground floor they emphasize snacks and izakaya, while upstairs there's a sushi island. Favorites: Sashimi that melts in your mouth and Toro tartare. Expansive whiskey selection. Their newly acquired highball machine makes tasty cocktails like the Suntory Whisky Toki highballs with grapefruit garnish.

MONTEVERDE
1020 W Madison St, Chicago, 312-888-3041
www.monteverdechicago.com
CUISINE: Italian
DRINKS: Full Bar
SERVING: Dinner; closed Mon
PRICE RANGE: $$$
NEIGHBORHOOD: West Loop

Stylish eatery offering a menu of contemporary Italian fare. The pastas here aren't great by accident. They make it all here. There's even a mirror over the pastificio (the table where they make the pasta) so you can watch. You'll see a cook stuffing tortelli with greens and ricotta cheese before they cook it and bring it to you. Special dishes such as Grilled octopus skewers and Duck egg ravioli. Reservations recommended.

MORRISON'S RESTAURANT AND CATERING
8127 S Ashland Ave, Chicago, 773-487-7000

https://www.allmenus.com/il/chicago/352006-morrisons-soul-food/menu/
CUISINE: Soul Food
DRINKS: No Booze
SERVING: Lunch, Dinner
PRICE RANGE: $$ / **cash only**
NEIGHBORHOOD: Auburn Gresham
Fair choice for comfort food like Mac 'n Cheese, ribs and cornbread. Daily specials. You go down a cafeteria line and point to the dishes you want. Just like the old days. Food iso only fair, not great. Avoid Sunday (unless you want to see everybody dressed to the nines), because you run into the after-church crowd. Cash only.

MOTT ST
1401 N Ashland Ave, Chicago, 773-687-9977
www.mottstreetchicago.com
CUISINE: Asian Fusion
DRINKS: Full Bar
SERVING: Dinner
PRICE RANGE: $$
NEIGHBORHOOD: Wicker Park
A lovely restaurant with an Asian street food-inspired menu. Menu favorites include: Whiskey-marinated pork neck, Crab Brain fried rice, and Oyster Mushrooms. Desserts include a Choco Banana, Mantou (yeasted doughnuts in chocolate) and Tres Leches Cake. A great dining experience especially if you share multiple plates.

NEXT
953 W Fulton Market, Chicago, 312-226-0858

www.nextrestaurant.com
CUISINE: Chinese/Steakhouse
DRINKS: Full Bar
SERVING: Dinner; closed Mon & Tues
PRICE RANGE: $$$$
NEIGHBORHOOD: West Loop
Upscale eatery popular among foodies who come for Grant Achatz's unique themed tasting menus. This dining experience completely changes every four months. It's a very exacting place, a little on the "too serious" side of the scale if you ask me, but if you're a diehard foodie, you'll want to put yourself through this experience. The unusual dishes here are unlike anything you've had elsewhere. This restaurant earned a James Beard Award as the Best New Restaurant in America.

NOMI
Park Hyatt Chicago
800 N Michigan Ave, Chicago, 312-239-4030

https://nomichicago.com
CUISINE: American with French influences
DRINKS: Full Bar
SERVING: Breakfast, Lunch, Dinner
PRICE RANGE: $$$$
NEIGHBORHOOD: Near North Side
It's hard to focus on the excellent food dished up here when you're glued to the captivating views from the seventh floor of the Park Hyatt Chicago, but force yourself. This elegant restaurant offers a simple menu featuring flavorful dishes made from regionally-sourced ingredients. Menu favorites include: Seafood salad, Pork belly with escargot, braised Jamison Farms lamb and Pork secreto. Nice wine and beer list and cocktail menu.

NORTH POND RESTAURANT
2610 N Cannon Dr, Chicago, 773-477-5845
www.northpondrestaurant.com
CUISINE: American
DRINKS: Full Bar
SERVING: Dinner
PRICE RANGE: $$$$
NEIGHBORHOOD: Lincoln Park
Located within the grounds of Lincoln Park, North Pond boasts one of the loveliest settings in the city. Set in a structure built in 1912 that was originally a warming shelter for ice skaters, Chef Bruce Sherman offers a creative seasonal menu of "upscale" New American cuisine. Menu favorites include: Grilled smoke sturgeon and Grass Fed Beef. Great tasting menu. Dessert choices include: chocolate mousse and cranberry sorbet.

ORIOLE
661 W Walnut St, Chicago, 312-877-5339
www.oriolechicago.com
CUISINE: American (New)
DRINKS: Full bar
SERVING: Dinner; closed Sun & Mon
PRICE RANGE: $$$$
NEIGHBORHOOD: Near West Side, West Loop
Intimate high-end eatery that's on everyone's must-visit list, this place serves top-notch New American dishes. Favorites: Kobe beef and Capellini pasta. Incredible dining experience. Crafted cocktails and specially baked desserts. **Note:** Reservations should be made months in advance if you hope to get a table.

OYSTER BAH
1962 N Halsted St, Chicago, 773-248-3000
www.oysterbah.com
CUISINE: Seafood
DRINKS: Full Bar
SERVING: Dinner; Lunch added Fri - Sun
PRICE RANGE: $$$
NEIGHBORHOOD: Lincoln Park
Here the menu focuses of fresh seafood including a mixture of classic and unique seafood dishes. Don't let the cute name throw you, or the tablecloths with the New England red checkerboard design. Or the nautical do-dads decorating the place. This place has great food. Thy usually offer 8 types of oysters, and you can have them fried, raw, grilled or broiled. I've had them each way and they are all excellent. Other

menu favorites: One-Sided Snapper, Stuffed Clam dish baked with chorizo. Small wine and cocktail list.

PARACHUTE
3500 N Elston Ave, 773-654-1460
www.parachuterestaurant.com
CUISINE: Korean
DRINKS: Full Bar
SERVING: Dinner
PRICE RANGE: $$$
NEIGHBORHOOD: North Side
Trendy eatery with red brick walls and low lighting (at night) help to project a friendly, even cozy ambience. Has a menu of creative Korean-American fare. Favorites: Pork Katsu with Napa cabbage; Dolsot bibimbap (with yellowfin tuna, smoked onion & lima beans); Ddukbokki (with pork and peach sofrito); and Broiled whole trout unagi style. Vegetarian and Gluten-free options.

PARSON'S CHICKEN & FISH
2952 W Armitage St, Chicago, 773-384-3333

www.parsonschickenandfish.com
CUISINE: American
DRINKS: Full Bar
SERVING: Lunch & Dinner
PRICE RANGE: $
NEIGHBORHOOD: Logan Square
Absolutely nothing fancy about this popular take-out spot selling fried chicken and fish. You can sit inside or outside. The grilled chicken is cooked Amish style (with citrus, scallions, rum, Habanero and spices), and you can get 2 pieces, a half chicken or a whole one. The fish fry comes with 3 piece, 6 pieces, or 9. The fish sandwich, however, is better, and comes with beer-battered fish, cole slaw and American cheese. (Get a side order of hush puppies.)

PASSEROTTO
5420 N Clark St, 708-607-2102
www.passerottochicago.com
CUISINE: Korean
DRINKS: Full Bar
SERVING: Dinner, Closed Sun & Mon
PRICE RANGE: $$$
NEIGHBORHOOD: Andersonville
Hip though still very casual eatery attracting a trendy crowd to its sleek interior with subdued lighting offering a menu of Korean fare with a few Italian influences. Four-course prix-fixe menu which is a good idea if you're not familiar with Korean cuisine. Favorites: Korean style tartare (rhubarb & white anchovies); Ddukbokki Lamb Neck Ragu with rice cakes; Kalbi Glazed Short Ribs & kimchi; Spare Ribs; Pork tenderloin.

PRIME & PROVISIONS
222 N La Salle St, Chicago, 312-726-7777
www.primeandprovisions.com
CUISINE: Steakhouse/Seafood/American (Traditional)
DRINKS: Full Bar
SERVING: Lunch & Dinner; Dinner only on Sat; closed Sun
PRICE RANGE: $$$$
NEIGHBORHOOD: The Loop

Located in a nearly 100-year-old building, this popular eatery celebrates true steakhouse cuisine. They dry-age the meat here on site. Great place for meat lovers looking for a great rib eye, Porterhouse, filet or steak. The bone-in Porterhouse for 2 costs over $100, but it's sure worth it. While they have all the usual steakhouse items, they have a few twists worthy of attention, like the crispy skinned fried chicken or the thick-cut bacon that looks more like a little pork chop than bacon. Great cocktails. Reservations recommended. Dessert? You gotta go for the banana cream pie.

PROST
2566 N Lincoln Ave, Chicago, 773-880-9900
www.prostchi.com
CUISINE: German/American Traditional
DRINKS: Full Bar
SERVING: Dinner, Lunch on Fri - Sun
PRICE RANGE: $$
NEIGHBORHOOD: Lincoln Park, DePaul
If you've ever been to a classic Bräuhaus in Munich, you'll feel right at home in this place in Lincoln Park. Typical German beer hall with a menu of traditional German fare. Great selection of beers including 24 draft beers (all German). Lots of TVs for sports fans. Try the Giant pretzel (enough for 4 to share).

PUB ROYALE
2049 W Division St, Chicago, 773-661-6874
www.pubroyale.com
CUISINE: Anglo/Indian
DRINKS: Full Bar
SERVING: Dinner; Lunch Fri - Sun
PRICE RANGE: $$
NEIGHBORHOOD: West Town – Wicker Park
Great pub with an impressive selection of tap beers and ciders. Despite the name "pub," it's known for excellent craft cocktails, and especially its "Royale Cups," their take on old standards like Pimm's Cup.

Very refreshing drinks, all of them (like the Tipple Royale Cup No. 1, which includes cucumber, strawberry, ginger beer & of course, that great drink that without which there would have been no Empire at all, Gin. Menu of Anglo-Indian pub fare including interesting dishes like eggplant curry, lamb dumplings, and chicken tikka roll. Great choice for weekend brunch.

THE PUBLICAN
837 W Fulton Market St, Chicago, 312-733-9555
www.thepublicanrestaurant.com
CUISINE: American
DRINKS: Full Bar
SERVING: Lunch (but late, opens at 3:30) & dinner nightly; weekend brunch from 10
PRICE RANGE: $$$
NEIGHBORHOOD: Fulton Market, Near West Side, West Loop

Known in these parts for their oysters, carefully selected pork, and beer. The menu is very much seasonal. Expect items like wild king salmon roe, smoked arctic char, duck hearts (with kale marmalade), blood sausages (among the best I've had), sucking pig, porchetta. There's even a daily pickle selection. They have a grilled chicken sauced with *piri piri* chile. He salts down the chicken a day before it's cooked, which makes it retain juices. Mouth-watering. They have a sticky bun bread pudding for dessert that's different and pleasing.

-This Little Piggy-
Winter food at The Purple Pig, Chicago

THE PURPLE PIG
444 N Michigan Ave, Chicago, 312-464-1744
www.thepurplepigchicago.com
CUISINE: Tapas/Mediterranean
DRINKS: Full Bar
SERVING: Lunch, Dinner
PRICE RANGE: $$
NEIGHBORHOOD: Near North Side
This is an intimate gastropub run by Jimmy Bannos Jr offering a tasting adventure for foodies. Here you'll find dishes you won't find anywhere else. Menu favorites include: Milk braised pork shoulder and Pork neck bone gravy with ricotta. There's also a great wine list and impressive offering of beers. Usually a long wait for tables. No reservations.

ROISTER
951 W Fulton Market, Chicago, 312-491-0058
www.roisterrestaurant.com
CUISINE: American (New)
DRINKS: Full bar
SERVING: Lunch & Dinner

PRICE RANGE: $$$
NEIGHBORHOOD: Fulton Market, Near West Side, West Loop

Located in the Fulton Market area, this hip eatery offers a menu of creative New American cuisine. This place has an unabashedly fun feel to it. Your flatware is tucked into a little pouch that will remind you of that "mess kit" you had when you went camping as a kid. The plates were crafted by a nearby an Illinois firm, Eshelman Pottery. The music played here started with a list of 900 songs sent in by everybody, but now they have about 3,000 songs. Favorites: Pasta & clams and Baked lasagna. Creative desserts.

RUSSIAN TEA TIME
77 E Adams St, Chicago, 312-360-0000
www.russianteatime.com
CUISINE: Russian

DRINKS: Full Bar
SERVING: Lunch, Dinner
PRICE RANGE: $$$
NEIGHBORHOOD: The Loop
One visit to this landmark Russian restaurant and you'll feel like part of the family. (Well, it might take two visits.) Typical Russian fare like Beef Stroganoff, Chicken Roulette, Ukrainian borscht, herring. Other regional cuisines represented are Uzbek, Azerbaijani and Moldavian. The Tea Service itself offers over 30 different teas, but that's not as important as the unusual pastries, sweets and other savories you get to choose from, including rugelach and Pozharski croquettes. Don't overlook the "vodka flights" that include various flavored vodkas. The wine selection, as you can imagine in a place like this, is wide ranging and carries labels you've never heard of.

SCHWA
1466 N Ashland Ave, Chicago, 773-252-1466
www.schwarestaurant.com
CUISINE: American
DRINKS: No Booze
SERVING: Dinner
PRICE RANGE: $$$$
NEIGHBORHOOD: Wicker Park
Here fine cuisine becomes a dining experience. Chef Michael Carlson serves up a menu of vivid courses featuring seasonal ingredients from around the world. A nine-course meal here is an unforgettable experience. Check out the tasting menu.

SIBLING'S SOUL FOOD
8127 S Ashland Ave, Chicago, 773-892-1078
https://www.allmenus.com/il/chicago/352006-morrisons-soul-food/menu/
CUISINE: Soul Food
DRINKS: No Booze
SERVING: Lunch, Dinner
PRICE RANGE: $$ / **cash only**
NEIGHBORHOOD: Auburn Gresham
Fair choice for comfort food like Mac 'n Cheese, ribs and cornbread. Daily specials. You go down a cafeteria line and point to the dishes you want. Just like the old days. Food iso only fair, not great. Avoid Sunday (unless you want to see everybody dressed to the nines), because you run into the after-church crowd. Cash only.

SHAW'S CRAB HOUSE
21 E Hubbard St, Chicago, 312-527-2722
www.shawscrabhouse.com
CUISINE: Seafood, Sushi Bar
DRINKS: Full Bar
SERVING: Lunch, Dinner
PRICE RANGE: $$$
NEIGHBORHOOD: Near North Side
Shaw's is actually two restaurants in one – a sophisticated seafood restaurant and an energetic oyster bar. Both offer a menu featuring top-grade fish and shellfish, oysters, and sushi and sashimi combinations. Menu favorites include the Maryland crab cake and the oysters (East and West Coast varieties). Bustling happy hour.

THE SMOKE DADDY
1804 W Division St, Chicago, 773-772-6656
www.thesmokedaddy.com
CUISINE: Barbeque
DRINKS: Full Bar
SERVING: Lunch, Dinner
PRICE RANGE: $$
NEIGHBORHOOD: Wicker Park
Barbecue sandwiches, down-home specials, and really loud music. Old time barbeque joint that serves barbeque chicken and pork, down-home specials, ribs, mac 'n cheese and even has a veggie burger. Interesting cocktails like the Bloody Mary garnished with meat. Live music. Known for its world famous Chicago BBQ sauce.

SMYTH AND THE LOYALIST
177 N Ada St. Ste 001, Chicago, 773-913-3773
www.smythandtheloyalist.com
CUISINE: American (New)/Seafood
DRINKS: Full Bar
SERVING: Dinner; closed Sun & Mon
PRICE RANGE: $$
NEIGHBORHOOD: Near West Side, West Loop
There are two distinct eateries here. Casual dining downstairs in what is called the Loyalist Pub, where you can get excellent pub grub like Burgers & Fries and Chicken wings. The burgers have bacon worked into the patties, so they're really delicious. You'll find the Loyalist Pub crowded after work as people pour in to relax. Upstairs at Smyth's you get 3 tasting menus (5, 8 and 12 courses) to choose from in a much fancier setting. The produce is grown specifically for

these two restaurants. Impressive selection of craft cocktails, craft beers and wines.

SOUTHPORT GROCERY & CAFÉ
3552 N Southport Ave, (betw. Addison St & Eddy St), Chicago, 773-665-0100
www.southportgrocery.com
CUISINE: American
DRINKS: Full bar
SERVING: Breakfast & Lunch (sometimes does dinner, but usually only Thursday and Friday—check to be sure)
PRICE RANGE: $$
NEIGHBORHOOD: Lakeview
A pioneer of the restaurant-plus-market concept, the chef and owner, Lisa Santos, still does it right. The airy, bright dining room has booth tables along the side wall and the staff's market picks on the blackboard: pork belly with Fat Toad Farm goat

milk caramel sauce from Vermont, feta from nearby Prairie Pure Farm. The eclectic menu is strong in grown-up kids' fare -- cupcake pancakes, stuffed French toast, grilled Brie sandwiches, artisanal Italian sodas -- and starred items are available in the grocery. Ms. Santos's kitchen also makes and packages a line of products for the market, including bread pudding pancake mix, granola and blueberry preserves.

SUPERDAWG DRIVE-IN
6363 N Milwaukee Ave, Chicago, 773-763-0660
www.superdawg.com
CUISINE: Hot dogs, Hamburgers
DRINKS: No Booze
SERVING: Lunch & Dinner
PRICE RANGE: $
NEIGHBORHOOD: Norwood Park
This is an iconic hot dog drive-in. Really fun to come here. They make their own hot dogs and serve piping hot fries that are out of this world. Everything on the menu is tasty but not if you're counting calories. The malts are the best. This is a drive-in. Limited indoor standing space. There are picnic tables when the weather is nice.

SUPERKHANA INTERNATIONAL
3059 W Diversey Ave, 773-661-9028
www.superkhanachicago.com
CUISINE: Indian/American (New)
DRINKS: Full Bar
SERVING: Dinner, Closed Sun & Mon.
PRICE RANGE: $$
NEIGHBORHOOD: Logan Square

Trendy eatery with nice textures used in the interior design, from the stone walls to the slanted wide beamed light wood ceiling to the open-air patio out back, all very nice. Offers an American twist on Indian street food. Favorites: Achaari Pork Pao and Butter Chicken Supreme. Lots of Vegetarian options here. Reservations recommended.

TAC QUICK THAI KITCHEN
1011 W Irving Park Rd, Chicago, 773-327-5253
www.tacquick.com
CUISINE: Thai
DRINKS: No Booze
SERVING: Lunch & Dinner
PRICE RANGE: $$
NEIGHBORHOOD: Wrigleyville
This top-notch Thai eatery features a creative menu with dishes like cookie-cutter curries and pad thais. Ask for the second menu where you'll discover items like the tart and smoky pork and rice sausage and ground chicken with crispy basil and preserved eggs. Check out the specials.

TANGO SUR
3763 N Southport Ave, Chicago, 773-477-5466
www.tangosur.net
CUISINE: Steakhouse; Argentine
DRINKS: No Booze; BYOB (no corkage fee)
SERVING: Dinner
PRICE RANGE: $$
NEIGHBORHOOD: Lakeview
This family-style Argentinean steakhouse, with two dining areas, serves delicious steaks. Large portions.

They have no alcohol but have a no corkage BYOB policy. Menu favorites include: Empanadas and Melted provolone served with red peppers; sliced eggplant served in vinegar; breaded beef Milanesa with 2 fried eggs on top; churrasco steaks, grilled half chicken; grilled short ribs served with sausages. Very busy and there's usually a wait.

TERZO PIANO
159 E Monroe St, Chicago, 312-443-8650
www.terzopianochicago.com
CUISINE: Italian
DRINKS: Full Bar
SERVING: Lunch
PRICE RANGE: $$$
NEIGHBORHOOD: The Loop
Located in the new Modern Wing of the Art Institute of Chicago, this is a great place for lunch or Sunday Brunch. Chef Tony Mantuano, known for his four-star Italian restaurant Spiaggia, uses fresh, organic,

and sustainably produced ingredients for his seasonal menus. Menu favorites include: Margherita pizza and Sausage flatbread. Nice wine list.

UNCLE MIKE'S PLACE
1700 W Grand Ave, Chicago, 312-226-5318
www.unclemikesplace.com
CUISINE: American/Filipino
DRINKS: No Booze
SERVING: Breakfast, Lunch
PRICE RANGE: $$
NEIGHBORHOOD: Ukrainian Village, West Town
Comfortable no-frills eatery. Menu offers all-day-breakfast and lunch. Their classic BLT is one of the best in town. Best Filipino breakfast food in Chicago. Try the Tocino and Bangus. Or the lugao, which is chicken and rice soup. They have a dish with spam and garlic rice that sounds terrible, but tastes great. Tea is free with your meal. The people here are very conscientious, and if you don't come back for the food, which you will, you will definitely want to visit these people again.

WHEREWITHALL
3472 N Elston Ave, 773-692-2192
www.wherewithallchi.com
CUISINE: American (New)
DRINKS: Full Bar
SERVING: Lunch, Dinner, Late night
PRICE RANGE: $$$
NEIGHBORHOOD: Avondale
Distressed ceiling gives the place a lot of character. Small intimate space is quite fun & charming. The

little patio out back is very nice, with its red brick wall and tilted fencing. This popular eatery offera a prix-fixe menu of 4-courses of New American fare. Favorites: Fresh trout and Skirt steak, but you never know what they'll serve till you get there. Nice wine pairings. I'd advise reserving ahead (for a table) because it's so small, but the bar doesn't take reservations, so you might try just walking in.

XOCO
449 N Clark St, Chicago, 312-661-1434
www.rickbayless.com
CUISINE: Mexican
DRINKS: Beer & Wine Only
SERVING: Lunch & Dinner; closed Sunday and Monday
PRICE RANGE: $$
NEIGHBORHOOD: Near North Side

Rick Bayless has a mini restaurant empire here in Chicago, and this is one of his stars. It's not fast food Mexican, but rapid enough to be confused as fast food. No question that it's good: churros fresh from the fryer. Empanada, Mexican hot chocolate (they grind the Mexican cacao beans in the front window), tortas (Mexican sub sandwiches), caldos (meal-in-a-bowl soups with veggies, seafood or pork belly). Only seats 40 and they don't take reservations, so plan on going early or late.

Chapter 5
NIGHTLIFE

ALLIUM RESTAURANT AND BAR CHICAGO
Four Seasons Hotel
120 E Delaware Pl, Chicago, 312-799-4900
www.alliumchicago.com
CUISINE: American
DRINKS: Full Bar
SERVING: Breakfast, Lunch, Dinner
PRICE RANGE: $$$
NEIGHBORHOOD: Near North Side
This is one of those classy hotel bars serving creative cocktails. If you get hungry there is a snack menu that

includes tasty treats like: Mushrooms n' Toast, Crispy Brussels Sprouts and Roasted Carrots.

THE AVIARY
955 W Fulton Market St, Chicago, 312-226-0868
www.theaviary.com
NEIGHBORHOOD: Fulton Market, Near West Side, West Loop
If you think you can just saunter up to the bar at the Aviary, think again. A limited number of reservations are accepted each day for seatings at 6, 8 and 10 p.m. Would-be patrons must e-mail their requests to reservations@theaviary.com. If selected, you will be contacted by 4 p.m. the day of the reservation. So much for advance planning. Owned by Chef Grant Achatz and his partner, Nick Kokonas, owners of celebrated Chicago restaurants like Alinea, this bar offers specialty cocktails that you won't find anywhere else, like the Tropic Thunder served in a specially designed glass called the porthole. Another specialty cocktail called the Ford's Model Tea Party is made with Ford's gin, Old Pulteney Scotch and Atsby Armadillo Cake vermouth, Mandarine Napoleon and Sicilian blood orange tea and is served in a china cup. Great list of beers from small brewers. A must-see for cocktail lovers.

BIG CHICKS
5024 N Sheridan Rd, (bet. Argyle St & Carmen Ave), Chicago, 773-728-5511
www.bigchicks.com
NEIGHBORHOOD: Uptown
There are so many clubs on Ontario Street, just north of the Loop, that it's sometimes known as Red Bull Row. To ease out of a troubled day, go to Big Chicks, a gay bar that welcomes everyone. The drinks are cheap, the crowd is friendly and the décor is nicely weird.

BILLY SUNDAY
3143 West Logan Blvd, Chicago, 773-661-2485

www.billy-sunday.com
NEIGHBORHOOD: Logan Square
A dark and charming craft-cocktail joint that serves creative cocktails befitting a chemist. Antique china and chandeliers make you feel like you're back in the 19th Century. There's also a delightful menu of excellent food.

BUDDY GUY'S LEGENDS
700 S. Wabash, Chicago, 312-427-1190
www.buddyguy.com
NEIGHBORHOOD: South Loop
Known as the nation's premier blues club, this club offers an impressive roster of local, national, and international blues acts. Some of the talents that have performed here include: Van Morrison, Willie Dixon, The Rolling Stones, Lou Rawls, David Bowie, John Mayer, Stevie Ray Vaughan, and The Pointer Sisters. Buddy Guy takes the stage every January with a series of sold out shows. Open 7 nights a week. Southern Cajun soul food menu available. Check website for schedule and prices.

CALIFORNIA CLIPPER BAR
1002 N California Ave, Chicago, 773-384-2547
www.californiaclipper.com
NEIGHBORHOOD: Humboldt Park
This is a restored cocktail lounge that's out of another era. Here you'll find board games instead of TVs. Chicago's only bar with grape soda in the gun. Live music Fridays and Saturdays. Monday night is Trivia Night. Cash only.

CH DISTILLERY & COCKTAIL BAR
564 W Randolph St, Chicago, 312-707-8780
www.chdistillery.com
NEIGHBORHOOD: Near West Side, West Loop
Distillery that also has a bar with a menu of shared plates like Duck tacos and Chicken wings. Here they distill vodka, gin, whiskey, bourbon and a few others. You can see the shining stills behind a glass wall. Crafted cocktails are created from their products. Tours available. This is a no-tip bar.

CHARLIE'S CHICAGO
3726 N Broadway St, Chicago, 773-871-8887
www.charlieschicago.com
NEIGHBORHOOD: Lakeview
Gay country themed dance club with the best in entertainment, 7 days a week. Charlie's Chicago offers a roster that includes: award-winning country programming, after-hours dance party, Bingo, Karaoke, and free dance lessons. Resident & Guest DJs and light shows. Open until 4 a.m. Cover charge.

THE CLOSET
3325 N Broadway St, Chicago, 773-477-8533
www.theclosetchicago.com
NEIGHBORHOOD: Lakeview
Open since 1978, this neighborhood bar, although known as a lesbian bar, welcomes everyone. A friendly joint with games like darts and video bowling. Free Wi-Fi. TVs feature sports and music videos. Karaoke on Thursday nights. Theme parties.

THE COMEDY BAR
500 N LaSalle Blvd, Chicago, 312 836 0499
www.comedybar.com/chicago/
NEIGHBORHOOD: Near North Side, River North
It offers performances on Fridays and Saturdays at 8 and 10 p.m. You won't find big names, but a hit-or-miss roster of itinerant comedians, some who heckle the audience in language that can't be printed here. Modest cover includes admission to the upstairs lounge, where bottle-service vodkas run $200 or more.

DRUMBAR at RAFFAELLO HOTEL
201 E Delaware Pl, Chicago, 312-933-4805
www.drumbar.com
NEIGHBORHOOD: Near North Side
Located on top of the **Raffaello Hotel**, this popular rooftop bar offers a menu of creative cocktails. There's an intimate indoor lounge and an outdoor terrace that offers beautiful views of Lake Michigan.

ELIXIR
3452 N Halsted, (bet. Newport Ave & Cornelia Ave), Chicago, 773-975-9244
www.elixirchicago.com
NEIGHBORHOOD: Lakeview
In Boystown, where you can easily find a place to sing show tunes, dance or screen "RuPaul's Drag Race," Elixir is a nice spot to relax. Specialty cocktails are big here.

EMPTY BOTTLE
1035 N Western Ave, Chicago, 773-276-3600
www.emptybottle.com
NEIGHBORHOOD: Ukrainian Village
This popular live music venue offers a schedule of local and independent music. Avant-garde bands play late at night, but Friday nights have morphed into a kind of country honky-tonk scene. Cash only. Menu features some great local breweries. It's a bit divey but friendly.

HAYMARKET PUB & BREWERY
737 W Randolph St, Chicago, 312-638-0700
www.haymarketbrewing.com
NEIGHBORHOOD: Near West Side
This pub features two separate areas – one for the bar and the other for dining. Guests can actually see the fermentation room where the beer is made. This place attracts an interesting crowd as it's the home of Chicago's Drinking & Writing Theater. Great beer selection with over 30 on tap. Appetizer menu available.

THE HIDEOUT
1354 W Wabansia Ave, Chicago, 773-227-4433
www.hideoutchicago.com
NEIGHBORHOOD: Noble Square
Open since 1934, this small music venue that looks like a dive bar is very prominent in Chicago's live music scene and offers a schedule of live music, theatrical performances, dance parties and comedy shows. Billed as "a regular guy bar for irregular folks who just don't fit in." Artists who have played here include Neko Case, Wilco and Mavis Staples. Check website for schedule.

HOUSE OF BLUES
329 N Dearborn St, Chicago, 312-923-2000
www.houseofblues.com/chicago
NEIGHBORHOOD: Near North Side
Whether you want a gospel brunch or a late-night jam fest, it's worth checking the schedule at House of

Blues Chicago, which has featured artists like the Who and Al Green. Popular music venue with locations all over the U.S. This venue attracts big-name performers from all genres including jazz, blues, gospel, alternative rock and hop-hop. Interior is a mix of blues bar and opera house. There's a second-stage in the restaurant offering live blues nightly. Check out the popular Sunday gospel brunch.

HYDRATE
3458 N Halsted St, Chicago, 773-975-9244
www.hydratechicago.com
NEIGHBORHOOD: Lakeview
Known as Chicago's Premier Gay Dance Club, offers a fun night featuring theme nights, drag shows and dancers. Cover Charge. Open 7 nights.

JAZZ SHOWCASE
806 S Plymouth Ct, Chicago, 312-360-0234
www.jazzshowcase.com
NEIGHBORHOOD: South Loop
Founded in 1947 by Joe Segal, this is the oldest jazz club in Chicago. The 170-seat venue offers a roster of some of the best jazz acts in Chicago. Some of the greats who have performed here include: Chris Potter, Frank Morgan, James Carter, Stu Katz, McCoy Tyner, Dexter Gordon, Richie Cole, Dizzy Gillespie, George Benson, and Joe Farrell. Check website for schedule and prices. Cover charge.

MILK ROOM
12 S Michigan Ave, Chicago, 312-792-3535
www.milkroomchicago.com

NEIGHBORHOOD: The Loop
Popular bar for fans of well-crafted cocktails made with unusual and rare ingredients. It's on the second floor of the Chicago athletic Association Hotel. Only 8 stools in here, and you have to reserve one. VERY expensive. Popular drinks: Old Scout Old Fashioned and the Whiskey Sour Redemption.

MURPHY'S BLEACHERS
3655 N Sheffield St (between Addison St & Waveland Ave), Chicago, 773-281-5356
www.murphysbleachers.com
NEIGHBORHOOD: Wrigleyville, Lakeview
Founded in the 1930s as Ernie's Bleachers, a hot dog stand hawking beer by the pail, Murphy's Bleachers is now a perpetually packed sports bar across the street from -- what else? -- the bleachers at Wrigley Field. Never mind that the Cubs haven't won a World Series since 1908. You can enjoy beers with the throngs who love them anyway.

REPLAY BEER & BOURBON
3439 N Halsted St, Chicago, 773-661-9632
www.replaylakeview.com
NEIGHBORHOOD: Boystown
Popular gay bar with a nice outdoor patio. Fills up late. Retro-feel with bar TVs, video games, jukebox and free popcorn. 25 beers on tap.

ROOF ON THE WIT
201 N State St, Chicago, 201 N State St, Chicago, 312 239 9502
www.thewithotel.com
NEIGHBORHOOD: The Loop
Upscale rooftop lounge located on the 27th floor of the Wit Hotel. Great summer scene. Creative cocktails and snack menu. Great spot for a first date when the weather permits.

ROSA'S LOUNGE
3420 W Armitage Ave, Chicago, 773-342-0452
www.rosaslounge.com
NEIGHBORHOOD: Logan Square
A family-owned blues lounge that features a variety of styles showcasing legendary singers like David Honeyboy Edwards, Homesick James and Pinetop.

ROSCOE'S
3356 N Halsted St, Chicago, 773-281-3355

www.roscoes.com
NEIGHBORHOOD: Lakeview
Since 1987, Roscoe's has been entertaining crowds. By day, it's a neighborhood bar with a sidewalk café but by night Roscoe's transforms into a lively nightclub with a great dance floor. Theme nights, drag shows, boy dancers, and Karaoke on Mondays & Wednesdays. Cover charge.

SCOFFLAW
3201 W Armitage Ave, Chicago, 773-252-9700
www.scofflawchicago.com
NEIGHBORHOOD: Logan Square
A popular neighborhood bar that serves great cocktails like Sly Devil made with Scofflaw Old Tom gin. The food is good too, particularly the burgers. There are tables but they're hard to come by and there's always a wait.

SIMON'S
5210 N Clark St, Chicago, 773-878-0894

NEIGHBORHOOD: Andersonville/Uptown
One of Chicago's old time favorite dive bars. Ok beer selection on tap and good Glogg. Juke box for music. Cash only.

SIDETRACK
3349 N Halsted St, Chicago, 773-477-9189
www.sidetrackchicago.com
NEIGHBORHOOD: Lakeview
A large gay video bar with five different bar areas on two-levels including a deck bar. Show tunes on the big screen, sing-along nights. Friendly crowd and staff.

THE VIOLET HOUR
1520 N Damen Ave, Chicago, 773-252-1500
www.thevioleth0ur.com

NEIGHBORHOOD: Wicker Park
This cocktail lounge may be difficult to find as there's no sign but it's worth the search. Inside there's a sign requesting that you refrain from using your cell phone. The décor is interesting with crystal chandeliers and beautiful hardwood floors giving the space a ballroom feel. The classic cocktails served are delish and strong but slow to come as the bartenders take great care in the preparation. Great atmosphere for drinking with friends.

WEEGEE'S LOUNGE
3659 W Armitage Ave, Chicago, 773-384-0707
www.weegeeslounge.com
NEIGHBORHOOD: Logan Square
An old-school cocktail lounge that does things their way, like making their own sour mix and ginger syrup. Here you'll find an impressive menu of beers (more than 100) with many coming from small

brewers. The bar is known for its glamorous, yet potent cocktails like the Aviation made from gin, fresh lemon juice, crème de violette and Luxardo maraschino liqueur. The bar also serves classic tunes ranging from Glenn Miller to Memphis Slim.

Chapter 6
WHAT TO SEE & DO

10 PIN BOWLING LOUNGE
330 N State St, Chicago, 312-644-0300
www.10pinchicago.com
NEIGHBORHOOD: Near North Side

A mega-bowling center featuring an upscale lounge. This 20,000 square-foot bowling center features 24 state-of-the-art lanes topped by 8 high-def video screens with a nightclub quality sound system. The center has plush sofas and intimate seating areas in the lounge and laneside tables for cocktails and dining while throwing the balls. This is a top of the line bowling destination and the home of the PBA Summer Shootout.

360 CHICAGO
HANCOCK OBSERVATORY
John Hancock Center, 875 N Michigan Ave, Chicago, 888-875-8439
www.jhochicago.com
NEIGHBORHOOD: Near North Side
Formerly **John Hancock Building Observation Deck**, 360 Chicago is located on the 94th floor of the historic John Hancock Center offering incredible views of the city and Lake Michigan. They have a

contraption called **Tilt**. You're strapped into a harness and then step into a glass enclosure which is then tilted over the city some 1,000 feet below. Not for me, thank you very much. But you might get a thrill out of it. The café and bar offer an ideal spot for cocktails while watching the sunset.

ADLER PLANETARIUM
1300 S Lake Shore Dr, Chicago, 312-922-7827
www.adlerplanetarium.org
NEIGHBORHOOD: Near Southside
ADMISSION: Modest admission fee
Open daily
Adler Planetarium features three-full-sized theaters: the Definiti Theater, the Samuel C. Johnson Family Star Theater, and the Grainger Sky Theater – the most technologically advanced theater in the world. This is the oldest planetarium in existence. Sky shows at all three theaters, exhibitions, and special lectures. Popular with young children who can simulate their own space missions.

ARCHITECTURE TOUR ON THE "L"
Chicago boasts some of the most interesting and varied 20th Century architecture in America. One neat (and cheap) way to see it all is aboard the L, the elevated train that gores around the Loop.

Simply get on at any station—doesn't matter if you're on the Pink, Orange or Brown line. The main thing is to grab a seat at the very front so you get to see the view of all the buildings you will pass by.

Over the course of the 2-mile trip, you'll see some of the best architecture Chicago has to offer, including Frank Gehry's Pritzker Pavilion band shell and Louis Sullivan's historic Auditorium Building, Bertrand Goldberg's spectacular Marina City, the new Trump International Hotel and Tower. Better yet, make the trip twice; your ticket (a couple of bucks) buys you an unlimited number of "loops."

THE ART INSTITUTE OF CHICAGO
111 S Michigan Ave, (bet. Adams St & Monroe St), Chicago, 312-443-3600
www.artinstituteofchicago.org
NEIGHBORHOOD: The Loop
Chicago knows how to mix neo-classical architecture with contemporary design, and no place does it better. The celebrated Modern Wing is an example of this. Designed by Renzo Piano, the luminous addition contains a magnificent set of galleries for 1900-1950. European art (Picasso, Giacometti, Klee are a few of the big names) and a cavernous room for the museum's well regarded design collection. (There's a spectacular rooftop restaurant called **Terzo Piano** that

offers splendid views of the Pritzker Pavilion in Millennium Park across the street.

BIKE & ROLL
239 E Randolph, Millennium Park (at Columbus Dr), Chicago, 312-729-1000
www.bikechicago.com
NEIGHBORHOOOD: The Loop
For around $35 a day you can peddle along the shore of Lake Michigan. You'll pass Navy Pier, skyscrapers by Mies van der Rohe, and hundreds of beach volleyball courts, which make this the Malibu of the Midwest on summer and fall weekends. Along the way, you'll pass Lincoln Park, with a new pavilion by the Chicago architect Jeanne Gang — another example of how the city is updating its open spaces.

BRIDGEHOUSE & CHICAGO RIVER MUSEUM
99 Chicago Riverwalk, Chicago, 312-977-0227
www.bridgehousemuseum.org
NEIGHBORHOOD: The Loop
A museum dedicated to Chicago's river and movable bridges. The museum offers a unique opportunity to visit the historic McCormick Bridgehouse. Starting at river level, you go up five stories. Once on top of the Bridgehouse, you'll get wonderful 360-degree views of the city and river. Modest fee. Closed Tuesdays and Wednesdays.

CHASE TOWER
10 S Dearborn St, Chicago, 312-732-1164
NEIGHBORHOOD: The Loop

A 60-story skyscraper completed in 1969. This is the tenth tallest building in Chicago and houses Chase Bank's U.S. and Canadian commercial and retail banking headquarters and the Exelon headquarters. The building occupies an entire city block. I only mention it because you should stop to have a look at Marc Chagall's "Four Seasons" in the plaza.

CHICAGO ARCHITECTURE CENTER
111 E Wacker, Chicago, 312-922-8687
www.architecture.org
NEIGHBORHOOD: The Loop
ADMISSION: Minimal admission fees per building
This organization celebrates and promotes Chicago as a center of architectural innovation. This organization offers many popular programs like the docent-led architecture cruise on the Chicago River as well as many bus, walking, bike, Segway and 'L' train tours of the Chicago-area. A must-see is the scale model of

downtown Chicago. CAF offers more than 85 tours of the city, many include historic buildings of Chicago. CAF hosts Open House Chicago, the largest annual architecture event in the city. CAF also offers an architecture and design education program.

CHICAGO BOTANIC GARDEN
1000 Lake Cook Rd, Glencoe, 847-835-5440
www.chicagobotanic.org
NEIGHBORHOOD: Glencoe
ADMISSION: Free, modest fee for parking.
A 385-acre living plant museum located on nine islands with 26 display gardens. The Garden features four natural habitats: McDonald Woods, Dixon Prairie, Skokie River Corridor, and Lakes and Shores. Open daily.

CHICAGO HISTORY MUSEUM
1601 N Clark St, Chicago, 312-642-4600
www.chicagohistory.org
NEIGHBORHOOD: Lincoln Park
Formerly known as the **Chicago Historical Society**, the museum was founded in 1856. The museum features exhibitions of Chicago and American history. The 16,000 square-foot space holds over 600 objects that document history including "The Pioneer," the first railroad locomotive in Chicago. They even have the actual bed where President Lincoln died after being shot at Ford's Theatre. Other exhibits include: Facing Freedom, Abraham Lincoln alcoves, and Sensing Chicago. Open 7 days. Nominal admission fee. Museum café and shop.

CHICAGO LINE CRUISES
465 McClurg Crt, Chicago, 312-527-1977
www.chicagoline.com
You get a unique perspective if you take in Chicago's buildings by boat. This tour exposes you to about 50 skyscrapers adjacent to the Chicago River.

CHICAGO SHAKESPEARE THEATER
800 E Grand Ave, Chicago, 312-595-5600
www.chicagoshakes.com
NEIGHBORHOOD: Near North Side
Located at Navy Pier, this non-profit, professional theater company offers more than six hundred performances annually. Programs include their Shakespeare series, World Stage touring productions, and summer programming for the family. The Courtyard Theater has 520 seats and offers state-of-the-art technology and acoustics. Check website for current production.

CHICAGO UNION STATION
225 S Canal St, Chicago, 800-872-7245
www.chicagounionstation.com
NEIGHBORHOOD: West Loop
Open since 1925, this is the third busiest rail terminal in the U.S. and the only intercity rail terminal in Chicago. This is one of Chicago's most iconic structures reflecting the strong architectural heritage. Notice the beautiful Bedford limestone Beaux-Arts facades, the massive Corinthian columns, the sparkling pink Tennessee marble floors and the impressive Great Hall. The Union Gallery, a beautiful 3,500 square-foot room that opens onto the Great

Hall, is often used for VIP receptions, lounges, and ceremonies.

CHICAGO TEMPLE
77 W Washington St #2, Chicago, 312-236-4548
www.chicagotemple.org
NEIGHBORHOOD: The Loop
The Chicago Temple Building is a landmark 568-foot Neo Gothic style skyscraper church and is home to the First United Methodist Church of Chicago. This is the tallest church building in the world and was the tallest building in Chicago until 1930. You can tour the Sky Chapel, 400 feet above street level, and see a statue of Jesus as he weeps over the city.

THE DRIEHAUS MUSEUM
40 E Erie St, Chicago, 312-482-8933
www.driehausmuseum.org
NEIGHBORHOOD: Near North Side

While shoppers mindlessly spend money only a few feet away on the Magnificent Mile, nearby is the most expensive private dwelling in Chicago when it was built. Located in one of the grandest buildings of 19th Century Chicago (built in 1883 for a rich banker named Samuel Nickerson), this museum celebrates historical preservation, having been converted into a museum by Richard Driehaus when he bought it in 2003. The galleries feature original furnishings along with pieces from the Driehaus Collection of Fine and Decorative Arts. The restored mansion features 17 types of marble, hand-painted ceilings, and carved exotic wood. Admission fee. Closed Mondays.

THE DUSABLE MUSEUM OF AFRICAN AMERICAN HISTORY
740 E 56th Pl, Chicago, 773-947-0600
www.dusablemuseum.org
NEIGHBORHOOD: Washington Park
ADMISSION: Minimal admission fee
Closed Mondays
Founded in 1961 by Dr. Margaret Godd Burroughs, this is the first and oldest museum dedicated to the study and conservation of African American history, culture, and art. The Harold Washington Wing features a permanent exhibition on his political career. Other notable highlights include: the desk of activist Ida B. Wells and the violin of poet Paul Laurence Dunbar. The museum's collection features 13,000 artifacts, books, photographs, art objects and memorabilia. The museum also feature prints and drawings of Henry O. Tanner, Richmond Barthé, and Romare Bearden.

FIELD MUSEUM
1400 S Lake Shore Dr, Chicago, 312-922-9410
www.fieldmuseum.org
NEIGHBORHOOD: Near Southside
ADMISSION: Modest admission fee
Open daily
A lot of people overlook this great place, so listen up: this is one of the largest natural history museums in the world with an amazing collection of high quality permanent exhibitions. The collections contain over 24 million specimens and objects with a full range of anthropological collections and artifacts from around the world. The Field Museum Library contains over 275,000 books, journals and photo archives.

FORK AND THE ROAD
2340 W Granville Ave, Chicago, 773-610-2432
https://forkandtheroad.com/
A unique concept that unites foodies and bike enthusiasts. Tour some of Chicago's most interesting neighborhoods by bike while visiting off-the-beaten-path food spots along the way. Taste food from some of the best restaurants and get to experience the neighborhoods at the same time. Tours begin near a bicycle rental facility for those without bikes. Reserve ahead. Fees include food samplings from pre-selected menus.

FREDERICK C ROBIE HOUSE
5757 S Woodlawn Ave, (bet. 57th & 58th Sts), Chicago, 312-994-4000
www.flwright.org/visit/robiehouse

NEIGHBORHOOD: Hyde Park
Robie House is a Frank Lloyd Wright masterpiece built between 1908 and 1910, the low-slung house is a U.S. National Historic Landmark and known as the greatest example of the Prairie School style. Audio and guided tours available for nominal fee. Closed on Tuesdays and Wednesdays.

THE GARFIELD PARK CONSERVATORY
300 N Central Park Ave, Chicago, 312-746-5100
www.garfieldconservatory.org
NEIGHBORHOOD: East Garfield Park
ADMISSION: FREE
Open daily
Known as "landscape art under glass," this is one of the largest conservatories in the U.S. The conservatory covers about 4.5 acres inside and out featuring thousands of plant species displayed in eight rooms. Inside you can experience the lush flora and

tropical temperatures all year round and the outdoor gardens during the summer. Exhibits include: the Fern Room, Sugar from the Sun, the Snow House, and the Elizabeth Morse Genius Children's Garden. The Aroid House features artist Dale Chihuly's 16 yellow lily pads on exhibit in the "Persian Pool" and the Desert House houses an impressive collection of cacti and succulents. Weekend activities for children are often scheduled.

GRANT PARK
337 E Randolph St, Chicago, 312-742-3918
www.chicagoparkdistrict.com
NEIGHBORHOOD: The Loop
Located in the central business district of Chicago, this urban 319-acre park hosts a variety of events including music festivals, plays and political speeches. The park is home to Millennium Park, the Art Institute, the Field Museum of Natural History and the Shedd Aquarium. The park is home to several performance venues, gardens, art works, sporting and harbor facilities.

HARRIS THEATER
205 E Randolph St, Chicago, 312-334-7777
www.harristheaterchicago.org
NEIGHBORHOOD: The Loop
Located along the northern edge of Millennium Park, the Joan W. and Irving B. Harris Theater for Music and Dance (also known as the Harris Theater) is a 1,525-seat theater for the performing arts. The theater is a venue for small and medium-sized music and dance groups including Joffrey Ballet, Hubbard Street

Dance Chicago and Chicago Opera Theater. Check website for current production.

INLAND STEEL BUILDING
30 W. Monroe Street, Chicago, 312-853-1550
www.inlandsteelbuilding.com
NEIGHBORHOOD: The Loop
The Inland Steel Building is a shining example of post-World War II era modern architecture. Built during the years 1956-57, this was the first skyscraper built in the Chicago Loop following the Great Depression.

INTERNATIONAL MUSEUM OF SURGICAL SCIENCE
1524 N Lake Shore Dr, Chicago, 312-642-6502
www.imss.org
NEIGHBORHOOD: Near North Side
This four-level museum celebrates medicine with exhibits of surgical instruments, paintings, and sculptures. Exhibits are old-fashioned but this is still a popular tourist attraction. Nominal fee. Closed on Mondays.

JACKSON PARK
6401 S Stony Island Ave, Chicago, 773-256-0903
www.chicagoparkdistrict.com/parks/jackson-park
NEIGHBORHOOD: South Side/Woodlawn
Bordering Lake Michigan and several South Side neighborhoods, this 500-acre park is home to over two-dozen species of birds, including the feral Monk parakeets. Frederick Law Olmsted, responsible for Central Park in New York, designed this park in the

1890s. He piled muck (dug up to create lagoons) onto a little hillock and ended up creating the 16-acre Wooded Island, which is still there. It was intended, as he put it, as "a place of relief from all the splendor and glory and noise and human multitudinousness of the great surrounding Babylon." If he could only see it now! The park is also home to the Museum of Science and Industry, the Osaka Garden – a Japanese strolling garden, the Chicago Landmark 63rd Street Bathing Pavilion, the 18-hole Jackson Park Golf Course, two walking trails, and two basketball courts.

KLUCZYNSKI FEDERAL CENTER
230 South Dearborn St, Chicago
NEIGHBORHOOD: The Loop
This modernist skyscraper is a 45-story structure designed by Ludwig Mies van der Rohe and completed in 1974. Named in honor of U.S. Congressman John C. Kluczynski. Constructed of a steel frame, it contains 1.2 million square-feet of office space. The entire center occupies two city blocks. That awkward thing in the plaza? That's Alexander Calder's "Flamingo" sculpture.

LINCOLN PARK ZOO
2001 N Clark St, Chicago, 312-742-2000
www.lpzoo.org
NEIGHBORHOOD: Lincoln Park
This world-class zoo was opened in 1868, and happens to be the oldest free public zoo in the country. You ought to carve out 2 or 3 hours to visit it. It has beautiful flowering gardens with walking paths, shade trees and Georgian Revival buildings.

Here they have more than 80 species of mammals, 70 species of reptiles, amphibians, and fish, and about 75 species of birds. Popular exhibits include the Kovler Penguin and Seabird House and the new Great Ape House. Open every day.

MILLENNIUM PARK
201 E Randolph St, Chicago, 312-742-1168
www.millenniumpark.org
NEIGHBORHOOD: The Loop
Open since 2004, this park was built to celebrate the Millennium, which perhaps accounts for its unglamorous name. Things being as they are, it wasn't finished until 4 years *after* the Millennium. Better late than never. The award-winning park features a state-of-the-art collection of architecture including the Jay Pritzker Pavilion, Cloud Gate, the Crown Fountain, and the Lurie Garden covering 5 acres that has to be seen to be believed. They have

dozens of free cultural programs (concerts, exhibitions and tours).

MONADNOCK BUILDING
53 W Jackson Blvd #850, Chicago, 312-922-1890
www.monadnockbuilding.com
NEIGHBORHOOD: South Loop
The Monadnock was the world's largest office building when it was built in 1893. The 16-story building was considered the world's first skyscraper.

MUSEUM OF CONTEMPORARY ART
220 E Chicago Ave (bet. Fairbanks Ct & Michigan Ave), Chicago, 312-280-2660
www.mcachicago.org
NEIGHBORHOOD: Near North Side, Streeterville. Contemporary art from around the world. Excellent location. Not yet known as one of the top art institutions in Chicago. They work hard to bring in excellent traveling exhibits, so always check their web site to see what they have going on now. They have one of the best museum gift shops in the country, however, worth a trip on its own, with a seriously eclectic collection of offerings. For instance, there's a duvet printed with an astronaut's spacesuit so your kid will look like he's wearing it when he's in bed. Another wacky item: for a mere $25, you can be the proud owner of a salt-and-pepper shaker featuring Marie Antoinette whose head is held on by a magnate. (Who thinks of things like this?) By the way, Wolfgang Puck has the food concession here where he serves moderately priced food (lunch only).

MUSEUM OF SCIENCE AND INDUSTRY
5700 S Lake Shore Dr, Chicago, 773-684-1414
www.msichicago.org
NEIGHBORHOOD: Hyde Park
ADMISSION: Moderate admission fee
This museum opened in 1933 during the Century of Progress Exposition and is the largest science museum in the Western Hemisphere. Exhibits include: a full-size replica of a coal mine, a German submarine, a 3,500-square-foot model railroad, the first diesel-powered streamlined stainless-steel passenger train, and the Apollo 8 spacecraft. The museum holds over 2,000 exhibits in 75 major halls. The museum has several free tours running through certain sections. The museum has many areas and is known for its unique exhibits like the walk-through model of the human heart, which has since been replaced with a 13-foot interactive, 3D heart. There's

also a recreation of a Chicago street from the early 20th century.

MUSIC BOX THEATRE
3733 N Southport Ave, Chicago, 773- 871 6604
www.musicboxtheatre.com
NEIGHBORHOOD: Lakeview
Open since 1929, this theatre has been the premiere venue in Chicago for independent and foreign films for over two decades. This is currently the largest theater space operating full time in Chicago. Check website for schedule.

NATIONAL MUSEUM OF MEXICAN ART
1852 W 19th St, Chicago, 312-738-1503
www.nationalmuseumofmexicanart.org
NEIGHBORHOOD: Pilsen
ADMISSION: FREE
Closed Mondays.
This is the only Latino museum accredited by American Alliance of Museums and the most prominent institution for Mexican art and culture in the U.S. Here you'll find one of the country's largest Mexican art collections boasting more than 7,000 pieces. The museum also host cultural programs including: symposia, theater, dance, music and lectures.

NAVY PIER
600 E Grand Ave, Chicago, 312-595-7437
www.navypier.com
NEIGHBORHOOD: Near North Side
ADMISSION: FREE. Attractions have separate fees
Open daily
Located on the Chicago shoreline of Lake Michigan, this 3,300-foot long pier was built in 1916 at a cost of $4.5 million. One of the most popular tourist attractions of the Midwest, the pier holds a variety of rides, restaurants, exhibitions, shops, and tours (cruises and boats). The 15-story Ferris wheel is one of the most popular attractions. Here you'll also find the Chicago Children's Museum located inside the Family Pavilion.

NORTH AVENUE BEACH
1600 N. Lake Shore Dr, Chicago, 312-742-PLAY
www.chicagoparkdistrict.com/parks-facilities/north-avenue-beach/

NEIGHBORHOOD: Lincoln Park
This popular beach features a unique ocean-liner inspired 22,000 square-foot beach house with a bar and bike rentals. Beach activities include running, biking, walking, volleyball, swimming, and rollerblading. One of the best places in the city to hang out in the summer.

OAK STREET BEACH
500–1550 Lake Shore Dr., 312 747 2474
www.chicagoparkdistrict.com/parks-facilities/oak-street-beach
This great beach opens in the summer from dawn to dusk. Besides swimming and getting a tan, people come here (by the thousands) to play beach volleyball or to cycle or skate along the paved pathways.
There's a not so well-known beach just to the south called
Milton Olive Park (named for a local Medal of Honor recipient).

OBAMA HOUSE
Walking around Hyde Park, a leafy enclave about seven miles south of the Loop, it's easy to see why the Obamas settled there. Their house, on South Greenwood Avenue between 50th and 51st Streets, is nearly invisible behind Secret Service barricades.

THE PEGGY NOTEBAERT NATURE MUSEUM
2430 N Cannon Dr, Chicago, 773-755-5100
www.naturemuseum.org
NEIGHBORHOOD: Lincoln Park
ADMISSION: Minimal admission fee
Open daily
Founded in 1999, this nature museum focuses on the natural history of the Chicago region. Exhibits include displays about the ecological history of the region, a live butterfly house (with more than 200 species of butterflies) and a green home

demonstration. More than 100 educational programs are offered for adults and children.

THE RANDOLPH STREET MARKET FESTIVAL
1341 W Randolph St, Chicago, 312-666-1200
www.randolphstreetmarket.com
NEIGHBORHOOD: Near West Side
This flea market has something for everyone and here you can find antiques, vintage estate jewelry and designer piece. Lots of vendors offering wares from cheap to expensive. Food vendors and live bands.

SHEDD AQUARIUM
1200 S Lake Shore Dr, Chicago, 312-939-2438
www.sheddaquarium.org
NEIGHBORHOOD: Near Southside
ADMISSION: Moderate ticket prices vary depending on experience
Once the largest indoor aquarium in the world, this aquarium contains over 25,000 fish with 5 million

gallons of water. This is the most visited aquarium in the U.S. Here you'll find over 1500 species including fish, marine mammals, birds, amphibians, insects, and snakes. Attractions include: Waters of the World, Caribbean Reef, Amazon Rising's Flooded Forest, Abbott Oceanarium, Wild Reef's Indo-Pacific Reef, Polar Play Zone and Shedd's Aquatic Show.

SHORELINE SIGHTSEEING
Chicago, 312-222-9328
www.shorelinesightseeing.com
Cruise around Chicago with friendly and knowledgeable guides.

TRIBUNE TOWER
435 N Michigan Ave, Chicago, 312-222-3994
This went up in 1925, and it's curious because inserted in the walls of this tower are rocks from many famous world landmarks, such as the Taj Mahal, the Parthenon, the Great Pyramid, the

Cathedral of Notre-Dame, the Great Wall of China, the Berlin Wall, and even the World Trade Center. They even have a rock from the moon. (Who thinks of things like this?)

THE UNIVERSITY OF CHICAGO'S ORIENTAL INSTITUTE
1155 E 58th St, Chicago, 773 702 9520
www.oi.uchicago.edu
NEIGHBORHOOD: Hyde Park
ADMISSION: FREE
Closed Mondays
Established in 1919, this museum and research center displays objects recovered by Oriental Institute digs from Egypt, Israel, Syria, Turkey, Iraq, and Iran. The Oriental Institute Museum is a world-renowned showcase for the history, art, and archaeology of the ancient Near East. The museum displays objects recovered by Oriental Institute excavations in permanent galleries devoted to ancient Egypt, Nubia, Persia, Mesopotamia, Syria, Anatolia, and the ancient site of Megiddo, as well as rotating special exhibits. Highlights of the collection include: the famous Megiddo Ivories, treasures from Persepolis, a collection of Luristan Bronzes and a large statue of King Tutankhamun.

WATER TOWER
Chicago Ave & Michigan Ave
The Gothic Revival façade of the Water Tower was only 2 years old when in 1871 Mrs. O'Leary's cow kicked over the lantern in her barn and caused the famous Fire. (Or so legend has it.) Today, along with the Pumping Station on the other side of the street, the Water Tower is the last visible reminder of the Old Chicago consumed by the devastating Great Fire. Surrounded by hotels and colossal department stores,

it's also the icon of the new city that arose. At night, the Water Tower is lit from within, and it's a memorable sight. Inside, the vintage machinery is long gone (along with the water), and the plain interior is occasionally used as a gallery space.

WALDORF ASTORIA SPA
11 E Walton St (bet. State St & Rush St), Chicago, 312-646-1310
www.elysianhotels.com
NEIGHBORHOOD: Near North Side
Located in the **Waldorf Astoria Chicago**, this 14,000 square-foot spa offers an impressive menu of personalized services as well as a nail spa, barber suite, relaxation areas and a fitness facility. Massages and facials are highlights on the menu of treatments available. Spa brochure can be downloaded online. Call ahead for reservations.

WRIGLEY FIELD
1060 W Addison St, Chicago, 773-404-2827
www.wrigleyfield.com
NEIGHBORHOOD: Wrigleyville, Lakeview
Home of the Chicago Cubs since 1916 and built in 1914, Wrigley Field has a capacity of 41,009 and is one of the greatest ballparks in America. When you walk into this hallowed space (you get the same feeling in Boston's Fenway Park), you realize why baseball was called the National Pastime, even if it's not that now. It's the oldest National League ballpark. Tours (game not included) are offered for a modest fee.

Chapter 7
SHOPPING & SERVICES

BLOWTIQUE
1 E Huron St, Chicago, 312-280-2400
www.blowtique.com
NEIGHBORHOOD: Near North Side
Featured in VOGUE's Best Dressed Issue, Blowtique has earned the reputation as Chicago's premier blow-out only salon.

BROADWAY ANTIQUE MARKET
6130 N Broadway, Chicago, 773-743-5444
www.bamchicago.com
NEIGHBORHOOD: Edgewater
Here you'll find Chicago's largest selection of vintage furniture, costume jewelry and fashions.

BRUNELLO CUCINELLI
939 N Rush St, Chicago, 312-266-6000
www.brunellocucinelli.com
NEIGHBORHOOD: Near North Side
Well known Italian brand for men and women's fashions. Here you'll find suits, shirts, jackets, and shoes.

CANDYALITY
835 N Michigan Ave, Chicago, 312-867-5500
www.candyality.com
Terese McDonald's third Chicago sweets emporium made its debut in December and features the 2,000-square-foot Life Is Sweet Museum, showcasing artwork made from candy and chronicling the city's history as America's candy manufacturing capital. In the space dedicated to the shop, an abundance of

bulk-candy bins shares space with more exclusive morsels like artful truffles named after local celebrities; prices, $1 to $50.

COLLETTI ANTIQUE POSTER GALLERY
49 E Oak St, Chicago, 312-664-6767
www.collettigallery.com
A gorgeous selection of Art Deco and Art Nouveau furniture and objects.

EDGEWATER ANTIQUE MALL
6314 N Broadway, Chicago, 773-262-2525
www.edgewaterantiquemall.com
NEIGHBORHOOD: Edgewater
Great shopping for the treasure hunter as this place carries antiques and vintage items from every era of the 20th Century including Art Deco, Modernist and Industrial. Here you'll find an ever-changing selection of furniture, accessories, art, jewelry, clothing, and collectibles. Over 45 dealers offering their wares.

GREEN CITY MARKET
Moving city market – check website for location
www.chicagogreencitymarket.org
NEIGHBORHOOD: Lincoln Park, Park at Wrigley, Peggy Notebaert Museum & Mary Bartelme Park
One of the best and widest ranging markets in America.

IKRAM
15 E Huron St (bet. State St & Wabash Ave), Chicago, 312-587-1000

www.ikram.com
NEIGHBORHOOD: Near North Side
A stylish boutique that counts Michelle Obama among its customers, with fashion-forward labels like Jason Wu and Martin Margiela.

INDEPENDENCE
47 E Oak St, 2nd Floor (bet. US Highway 41 & Rush St), Chicago, 312- 675-2105
www.independence-chicago.com
NEIGHBORHOOD: Near North Side; West Loop
George Vlagos is one of the few retailers in Chicago that carries Engineered Garments, Imogene + Willie denim. An elegant men's shop featuring all-American made brands like Left Field, Velva Sheen, Engineered Garments, and Post Overalls.

INTELLIGENTSIA COFFEE
53 W Jackson Blvd, Chicago, 312-253-0594
www.intelligentsiacoffee.com
NEIGHBORHOOD: The Loop
Popular specialty coffee shop with several locations in Chicago. This one has the advantage of being in the elegant **Monadnock Building**, considered to be

the world's first "skyscraper" when it was built in 1893.

LUXURY GARAGE SALE
900 N Michigan Ave, 833-547-5470
www.luxurygaragesale.com
NEIGHBORHOOD: Lincoln Park
Two childhood friends, Brielle Buchberg and Lindsay Segal, started this unique concept – an upscale consignment boutique that offers new and gently used designer and vintage clothing and accessories with personalized service.

OPTIMO
51 W Jackson Blvd, Chicago, 312-922-2999
www.optimo.com
NEIGHBORHOOD: The Loop
The ultimate hat shop for men. They measure your head and custom make your hat. Wide variety of custom and ready-to-wear hats – everything from fedoras to derbies.

PAVILION
2055 N Damen Ave, Chicago, 773-645-0924
www.pavilionantiques.com/
NEIGHBORHOOD: Bucktown
Here you'll find an amazing selection of 20th century decorative arts and furnishings with an emphasis on French, Italian and Scandinavian. Collectors love this place for its well-edited collection of antique and contemporary pieces including furniture, lamps, mirrors, and sculptural accents.

PERMAN WINE SELECTIONS
1167 N Howe St, Chicago, 312-255-8990
www.permanwine.com
NEIGHBORHOOD: Near West Side
This is the most unique and attractive wine shop in Chicago. Here you'll get great service and often the owner is on hand to help you with your selection. This store also offers wine tastings and seminars.

PUBLICAN QUALITY MEATS
825 W Fulton Market St, Chicago, 312-445-8977
www.publicanqualitymeats.com
NEIGHBOORHOOD: Near West Side, West Loop
An incredible butcher shop serving up some of the best artisanal breads, handcrafted charcuterie, sandwiches, and fresh porchetta in town. Lunch for two will run about $30.

SPROUT SAN FRANCISCO
1943 W Division St, Chicago, 773-489-0009
www.sproutsanfrancisco.com
NEIGHBORHOOD: Ukrainian Village
A natural and organic children's boutique offering everything needed to create a healthy home for your child. Chemical free products.

SUITSUPPLY
945 N Rush St, Chicago, 312-874-5772
www.suitsupply.com
NEIGHBORHOOD: Near North Side
An elegant men's shop that offers European suits tailored while you wait, a wall of silk ties in every

color, and beautiful shirts. Here you'll be treated like a king and dressed like a prince.

QUIMBY'S BOOKSTORE
1854 W North Ave, Chicago, 773-342-0910
www.quimbys.com
NEIGHBORHOOD: Wicker Park
This local bookstore offers a variety of books, zines, comic books and magazines with markdowns in a little nook in the back. Here you'll find works of both mainstream and local authors. Check website for author readings/signings.

WRIGHT
1440 W Hubbard St, Chicago, 312-563-0020
www.wright20.com
NEIGHBORHOOD: Near West Side
This is a premier auction house that specializes in modern and contemporary design. This is a favorite of collectors looking for design pieces and fine art. Pieces offered range from Eames chairs to canvases by George Condo and Kenny Scharf.

INDEX

1

10 PIN BOWLING LOUNGE, 93

3

360 CHICAGO, 94

A

ACME HOTEL COMPANY, 14
ADLER PLANETARIUM, 95
ALINEA, 27
ALLEGRO, 14
ALLIUM RESTAURANT AND BAR, 79
American (New), 28, 31, 42
American Traditional, 64
Anglo, 65
ANN SATHER, 28
ARBOR, 28
ARCADIA, 29
ARCHITECTURE TOUR ON THE "L", 95
ART INSTITUTE, 96
ARTOPOLIS BAKERY & CAFE, 30
Asian Fusion, 44
ASTORIA, 24
ATWOOD CAFÉ, 31
AU CHEVAL, 31
AVEC, 32
AVIARY, 80

B

BAD HUNTER, 32
BAKERY AT FAT RICE, 33
BERGHOFF, 33
BEST WESTERN HAWTHORN TERRACE, 15
BIG CHICKS, 81
BIG JONES, 34
BIG STAR, 35
BIKE & ROLL, 97
BILLY GOAT TAVERN, 36
BILLY SUNDAY, 81
BLACKBIRD, 36
BLEACHERS, 88
BLOWTIQUE, 121
Brazilian, 52
BRIDGEHOUSE & CHICAGO RIVER MUSEUM, 97
BROADWAY ANTIQUE MARKET, 121
BRUNELLO CUCINELLI, 122
BUDDY GUY'S LEGENDS, 82

C

CAFÉ MARIE- JEANNE, 37
CALIFORNIA CLIPPER BAR, 82
CANDYALIT, 122
CELLAR DOOR PROVISIONS, 38
CESAR'S RESTAURANT, 38

CH DISTILLERY & COCKTAIL BAR, 83
CHARLIE'S CHICAGO, 83
CHASE TOWER, 97
CHICAGO ATHLETIC ASSOCIATION HOTEL, 15
CHICAGO BOTANIC GARDEN, 99
CHICAGO CHOP HOUSE, 39
CHICAGO DINER, 40
Chicago Historical Society, 99
CHICAGO HISTORY MUSEUM, 99
CHICAGO SHAKESPEARE THEATER, 100
CHICAGO TEMPLE, 101
Chinese, 44, 59
CITY MOUSE, 41
CITY SUITES, 16
CLOSET, 83
COALFIRE PIZZA, 41
COLLETTI, 123
COMEDY BAR, 84
Commons Club, 24
CONTEMPORARY ART, 109
CORRIDOR BREWERY & PROVISIONS, 41

D

DRAKE, THE, 16
DRIEHAUS MUSEUM, 101
DRUMBAR, 84
DRYHOP BREWERS, 42
DUSABLE MUSEUM OF AFRICAN AMERICAN HISTORY, 102
DUSEK'S, 43

E

EDGEWATER ANTIQUE MALL, 123
ELIXIR, 85
ELSKE, 43
ELYSIAN SPA AND HEALTH CLUB, 119
EMPTY BOTTLE, 85

F

FAT RICE, 44
FIELD MUSEUM, 103
FLORIOLE CAFÉ & BAKERY, 45
FORK AND THE ROAD, 103
FREDERICK C ROBIE HOUSE, 103
FREEHAND HOSTEL AND HOTEL, 17
French, 52
FRONTERA GRILL, 45

G

GALIT, 46
GARFIELD PARK CONSERVATORY, 104
GIANT, 47
GIBSONS BAR & STEAKHOUSE, 47
GILT BAR, 48
GIRL & THE GOAT, 49
GODFREY HOTEL CHICAGO, 17
GOOD FORTUNE, 49
GRANT PARK, 105
GREEN CITY, 123
GT FISH & OYSTER, 50

H

HAMPTON INN CHICAGO DOWNTOWN, 18
HANCOCK OBSERVATORY, 94
Hancock Tower, 6
HARRIS THEATER, 105
HAYMARKET PUB & BREWERY, 85
HIDEOUT, 86
HONKY TONK BARBEQUE, 51
HOTEL LINCOLN, 18
HOUSE OF BLUES, 86
HOXTON, 19
HYATT PLACE CHICAGO/DOWNTOWN, 19
HYDRATE, 87

I

IKRAM, 123
INDEPEDENCE, 124
Indian, 65
INLAND STEEL BUILDING, 106
INTELLIGENTSIA COFFEE, 124
INTERNATIONAL MUSEUM OF SURGICAL SCIENCE, 106
Italian, 57

J

JACKSON PARK, 106
JAM, 51
JAZZ SHOWCASE, 87
John Hancock Building Observation Deck, 94

K

KLUCZYNSKI FEDERAL CENTER, 107

L

LA SERENA CLANDESTINA, 52
LANGHAM, 20
Latin American, 52
LES NOMADES, 52
LINCOLN PARK ZOO, 107
LINE CRUISES, 100
LITTLE GOAT BREAD, 53
LOEWS CHICAGO HOTEL, 21
LONGMAN, 53
LUXURY GARAGE SALE, 125

M

MAJESTIC HOTEL, 21
MAUDE'S LIQUOR BAR, 54
MI TOCAYA ANTOJERIA, 55
MIA FRANCESCA, 56
MILK ROOM, 87
MILLENNIUM, 108
Milton Olive Park, 113
MOMOTARO, 56
Monadnock Building, 124
MONADNOCK BUILDING, 109
MONTEVERDE, 57
MOTT ST, 58
MUSEUM OF SCIENCE AND INDUSTRY, 110
MUSIC BOX THEATRE, 111

N

NATIONAL MUSEUM OF MEXICAN ART, 111
NAVY PIER, 112
NEXT, 58
Nico Osteria, 23
NOMI, 59
NORTH AVENUE BEACH, 112
NORTH POND, 60

O

OBAMA HOUSE, 114
OPTIMO, 125
ORIOLE, 61
OYSTER BAH, 61

P

Palm Court, 17
PARACHUTE, 62
Park Hyatt Chicago, 59
PARK HYATT CHICAGO, 21
PARSON'S CHICKEN & FISH, 62
PASSEROTTO, 63
PAVILION, 125
PEGGY NOTEBAERT NATURE MUSEUM, 114
PERMAN WINE SELECTIONS, 126
PRIME & PROVISIONS, 64
PROST, 65
PUB ROYALE, 65
PUBLICAN, 66
PUBLICAN QUALITY MEATS, 126
PURPLE PIG, 67

Q

QUIMBY'S BOOKSTORE, 127

R

Raffaello Hotel, 84
RANDOLPH STREET MARKET FESTIVAL, 115
RENAISSANCE BLACKSTONE, 22
REPLAY BEER & BOURBON, 88
ROISTER, 67
ROOF ON THE WIT, 89
ROSA'S LOUNGE, 89
ROSCOE'S, 89
RUSSIAN TEA TIME, 68

S

Salone Nico, 23
SCHWA, 69
SCOFFLAW, 90
Seafood, 61, 64
Shag Room, 24
SHAW'S CRAB HOUSE, 70
SHEDD AQUARIUM, 115
SHORELINE SIGHTSEEING, 116
SIBLING'S SOUL FOOD, 70
SIDETRACK, 91
Signature Room, 6
SIMON'S, 90
SMOKE DADDY, 71
SMYTH AND THE LOYALIST, 71
SOHO HOUSE CHICAGO, 22
Soul Food, 58, 70
SOUTHPORT, 72
SPROUT SAN FRANCISCO, 126
Steakhouse, 59, 64

SUITSUPPLY, 126
SUPERDAWG DRIVE-IN, 73
SUPERKHANA INTERNATIONAL, 73

T

TAC QUICK THAI KITCHEN, 74
TANGO SUR, 74
Terzo Piano, 96
TERZO PIANO, 75
THOMPSON CHICAGO, 23
Tilt, 95
TRIBUNE TOWER, 116

U

UNCLE MIKE'S PLACE, 76
UNION STATION, 100
UNIVERSITY OF CHICAGO'S ORIENTAL INSTITUTE, 117

V

VIOLET HOUR, 91
VIRGIN HOTEL CHICAGO, 23

W

Waldorf Astoria Chicago, 119
WATER TOWER, 118
WEEGEE'S LOUNGE, 92
WHEREWITHALL, 76
WILLOWS HOTEL, 25
WRIGHT, 127
WRIGLEY FIELD, 120

X

XOCO, 77

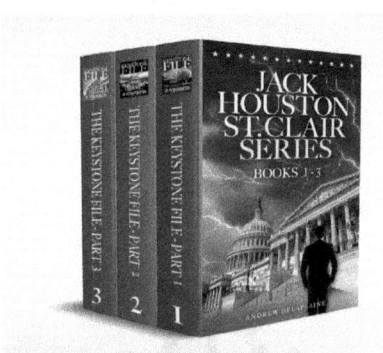

WANT 3 FREE THRILLERS?

Why, of course you do!

If you like these writers--
Vince Flynn, Brad Thor, Tom Clancy, James Patterson, David Baldacci, John Grisham, Brad Meltzer, Daniel Silva, Don DeLillo

If you like these TV series –
House of Cards, Scandal, West Wing, The Good Wife, Madam Secretary, Designated Survivor

You'll love the **unputdownable** series about Jack Houston St. Clair, with political intrigue, romance, suspense.

Besides writing travel books, I've written political thrillers

for many years that have delighted hundreds of thousands of readers. I want to introduce you to my work!
Send me an email and I'll send you a link where you can download the first 3 books in my bestselling series, absolutely FREE.

Mention **<u>this book</u>** when you email me.

andrewdelaplaine@mac.com

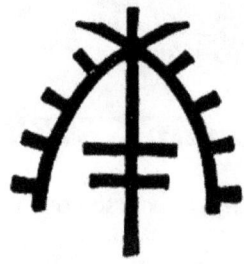